Golden Rules
for Living Your
Best Life

Swami Mukundananda is a world-renowned spiritual teacher from India, an international authority on mind management and a bestselling author. He earned his degrees from the prestigious IIT-D and IIM-C but chose to enter monkhood, renouncing a promising corporate career. He studied the Vedic scriptures at the feet of Jagadguru Kripaluji Maharaj. For almost four decades now, he has been sharing his vast knowledge through his books, lectures and life-transformation programmes.

Every day, Swamiji meets hundreds, and even thousands, of people from all walks of life. His steadfast positivity exudes hope, clarity and a sense of purpose to those who connect with him. He has deeply affected the lives of millions of people who have been drawn by his profound integrity, charismatic personality and passion to serve. Despite his busy schedule, those who encounter him experience his genuinely caring and compassionate personality and feel deeply touched by him. Swamiji's lectures are humorous, his arguments are logical and well laid-out, and most of all, his advice is practical. His lectures on social media platforms are loved and followed by millions. Swamiji divides his time between India and the US.

swamimukundananda.org
facebook.com/Swami.Mukundananda
instagram.com/Swami_Mukundananda
twitter.com/Sw_Mukundananda
youtube.com/c/swamimukundananda
linkedin.com/in/swamimukundananda

Praise for the Book

Golden rules for living your best life have been presented in this book by Swamiji with his patent flair for precision and ease. Practical solutions to complex challenges of life have been written with beguiling simplicity. And they cover the gamut of life, from material to the deepest spiritual. The book gives us tools to live our best physical, professional, financial, emotional and spiritual life. It's a comprehensive handbook for steadily moving towards our best version.

—Bhavna Roy and Amish Tripathi, bestselling authors

This book is truly a masterpiece. It is the perfect amalgamation of in-depth study of scriptures, regular introspection, human relations and *guru kripa*. The more you read, the more you attain clarity on how to integrate values and morals to create intrinsic and extrinsic harmony. The manner in which the author seamlessly integrates his personal experiences is remarkable. This further enhances the validity of the authorship and aids in reiteration, retention and consolidation of the concepts. Each and every line filled with an abundance of knowledge and wisdom proves that the author possesses a deep understanding of the purpose of life. By understanding the concepts in this book, one will be encouraged to create their own inner utopia. If you are interested in the purpose of life, this book is a perfect guide!

—Mahamahopadhyaya Swami Bhadreshdas, Head, BAPS, Swaminarayan Research Institute, Akshardham, New Delhi

A deeply spiritual book written with heart-touching simplicity. Reading this will bring harmony to our lives.

—Anand Neelakantan, Indian author, columnist, screenwriter and public speaker

Any book by Swami Mukundanandaji is a gem. Each page reveals profound and insightful workings of the human mind, addressing 'How to' questions about life. There is outstanding integration of knowledge filled with love, holistic solutions and an empowerment package to live a simple, peaceful and healthy life. Swamiji has blended his wisdom, science and spiritual technology in a logical step-by-step manner. It is a total transformation package, a toolkit. Use any tool from the book to make you healthier and happier.

Hands down—fantastic!

—Nick Shroff, MD, ERYT, Chairman,
American Association of Physicians of Indian Origin (AAPI),
USA

In this eminently readable book, Swamiji's wisdom is provided in bite-sized chapters which, in his signature style, bestow a touch of grace upon the pragmatic aspects of life. The practical and the sublime come together wonderfully in this guide to living one's best life, in our fractured, hectic times.

—Devapriya Roy, bestselling author

There is a common perception that the five facets of a well-lived life—good health, professional success, harmonious relationships, financial stability and spirituality—are mutually exclusive. Any progress in one facet can only be achieved by compromising the other facets. However, Swamiji has clearly established using irrefutable logic and real-world examples how each facet can be used as a force multiplier to propel others. The book has practical tools, techniques and methods for achieving cohesive growth across all the five aspects.

A must-read for all at whatever stage one may be in life.

—Harish Rangacharya, CEO, Apex Group, Virginia, USA

Imagine you are travelling to a new place and find yourself at a crossroads and don't know which road to take ahead. If you take the wrong way, you will never reach the destination. Take the right road and you will be successful and happy. Now imagine a local person comes along, and you ask him which way to take. He not only shows you the direction but also tells you how to avoid the pitfalls in the journey. He also hands over a bottle of water to quench the thirst on the way.

Swamiji is one such guide in our journey called Life. In this book, he answers all our questions that we would come across at the crossroads of life. Be it spiritual, professional or health issues, this book touches upon and answers all questions we come across. Not only read the book but also make it your ready reference manual forever.

You already have found your guide and mentor for life in this book.

—Dr Radhakrishnan Pillai,
bestselling author of the *Chanakya* series

Humans are not born with a manual for life. Fortunately, God graces us with parents, teachers, friends and colleagues, who can potentially mentor us. However, it is extremely rare to find genuine and unconditional guidance.

While the grace of a living Guru tends to be for a select few, through this book, Swamiji has ensured that such grace extends to millions. He has causelessly showered His energy to provide bona fide and pragmatic wisdom in this book that can enrich one's life. It underscores the lesser-known path for a successful and meaningful life.

—P. Surya Prakash, Managing Director,
SatyaVani Projects and Consultants Pvt. Ltd, Hyderabad

This book is a treasure trove as it explores all facets of human life from the basic question of purpose of life to understanding and changing beliefs to overcoming fear, resentment and anger to achieving success at work while maintaining a healthy lifestyle. In his landmark writing style, with knowledge culled from the Eastern and Western scriptures alike, Swamiji integrates one's basic material dharma with the higher spiritual dharma for a balanced life. The end result is this one-of-a-kind book which is a manual for life. It is like a North Star to smoothly navigate through the turbulent sea of life.

Unlike other spiritual leaders, Swamiji does not shy away from addressing the various facets of the material world. Instead, he takes the bull by the horns and addresses the basic issues of the material world like wealth management, happy relationships and professional fulfilment, head-on.

Swamiji does not attempt to teach or preach, but instead, encourages the reader to explore, enquire and discover solutions to life's challenges. You might not be able to change what Life throws at you, but this book will empower you to accept, adapt and face the obstacles with courage and conviction.

It is a powerful, once-in-a-lifetime literary work that will influence humanity, shape society and make this world a better place.

—Major General Anoop Kumar V. (Retd), Sena Medal

Golden Rules
for Living Your
Best Life

Swami Mukundananda

RUPA

First published by
Rupa Publications India Pvt. Ltd 2022
7/16, Ansari Road, Daryaganj
New Delhi 110002

Sales Centres:
Prayagraj Bengaluru Chennai
Hyderabad Jaipur Kathmandu
Kolkata Mumbai

The views and opinions expressed in this book are the author's own and the
facts are as reported by him which have been verified to the extent possible,
and the publishers are not in any way liable for the same.

P-ISBN: 978-93-5520-788-3
E-ISBN: 978-93-5520-789-0

Fifth impression 2023

10 9 8 7 6 5

The moral right of the author has been asserted.

Printed in India

This book is dedicated to my beloved Spiritual Master, Jagadguru Shree Kripaluji Maharaj, the embodiment of divine love and grace, who illuminated humankind with the purest rays of divine knowledge. He was immersed in the highest bliss of divine love and engaged in inundating the entire planet with it. I am eternally indebted to him for bestowing upon me his divine wisdom and for inspiring me to consecrate my life to its propagation. I pray that by his blessings this book will help sincere seekers live a successful life.

Contents

Introduction

We all share the same aspirations. We hope to achieve perfect happiness, true love and well-being. Unfortunately, life presents us the reverse, and we find difficulties, disheartenments and failures on our platter. The challenges are further compounded, since situations present themselves first, while the wisdom for handling them is learnt later.

Every complex gadget comes with its user's manual. It is a one-stop resource for learning how to use the device, and what to do in case of problems. Would it not be nice if there were a manual for life as well? We could then reverse the sequence of problems and solutions, to equip ourselves in advance with precious wisdom.

Imagine purchasing your first computer, with no guidebook for using it. How long and difficult the learning curve would be! The dilemma of life is similar. With no prior training, we are expected to make good choices and adopt best strategies. Thus, learning comes the hard way—through bitter experiences—or not at all. It is like being thrown in the deep end of the pool without knowing how to swim.

This book aims at bridging that gap. It will equip you with the knowledge you need for successfully negotiating your sojourn in the world.

Why this book was written. Let me share with you a moment of personal epiphany.

As a spiritual teacher in the renounced order since the last four decades, I have engaged in all kinds of social work and have seen them succeed to a lesser or greater extent. A defining moment in my endeavours came 30 years ago, when I asked my Spiritual Mentor, 'Maharajji, what is the best way in which we can help people around the globe?'

Gurudev's answer was extremely enlightening. He said, 'The biggest service you can do is to illumine people with true knowledge. Show them the way to achieve everlasting happiness, find genuine love and get rid of suffering.'

His answer hit the nail on the head. The biggest calamity on this planet is the immense untapped human potential of billions of people. And the primary reason for it is the lack of awareness of processes, tools and techniques to unleash it. Hence, the Bhagavad Gita states:

na hi jñānena sadṛiśhaṁ pavitramiha vidyate   (4.38)

'In this world, there is nothing as purifying as divine wisdom.' The Gita teaches us to seat ourselves on the boat of divine knowledge and sail over the ocean of life and death.

Even one little gem of wisdom can create a paradigm shift in our life. A single health tip could work wonders and make you well. One bit of guidance from your professional mentor may well turn your career around. A few words of advice from your spiritual guide can transform your life forever. Then what to speak of a treasure chest of wisdom? The aim of this book is to help you learn several hundred such gems of knowledge for enhancing the quality of your life.

Such a meaningful and enriched life requires upgrading its key critical areas. These are:
- Spiritual and emotional wellness,
- Good health and well-being,
- Harmony in relationships,
- Professional fulfilment, and
- Financial abundance.

If you can effectively manage these five dimensions of your existence, the other aspects automatically get elevated.

Authenticity of the wisdom shared. Some people make management science the object of their study, while others focus on learning economics or sociology. My passion has always been to study wisdom related to life itself. For that, over the years, I have culled insights from thousands of scriptures and books of wisdom from around the world.

In the process of teaching spirituality, I have had the opportunity to explain the perennial knowledge of the Vedas to millions of wonderful souls from various countries. While counselling them, I have gotten into their shoes to understand how they think and have helped them resolve their issues. The feedback they have shared has been a constant learning for me. In my own journey as a student and a teacher, I have struggled and faltered numerous times and always grown wiser as a result. This book is the ripened fruit of that cumulative wisdom.

Synthesis of science and spirituality. Very often, we observe neophyte spiritualists condemning material knowledge and hardcore materialists denouncing spiritual science. However, the *Atharva Veda* states:

dve vidye veditavye...parā chaivāparā cha

(*Mundakopanishad* 1.1.4)

'To triumph at life, you must possess both spiritual and material wisdom.' This book is enriched with a judicious blend of the wisdom from both these realms.

This is also the principle behind the JKYog method of holistic wellness, also called 'Yoga for the Body, Mind and Soul'. This health system includes yogic postures, pranayam, relaxation techniques, meditation and the science of healthy diet. Together, these practices help develop and maintain the physical, emotional, intellectual and spiritual dimensions of our personality. In the health section of this book, I have distilled insights from these sciences for healthy living and wellness.

Every day, I am approached by individuals, families, groups and organizations looking for guidance and solutions. I hope this book will serve them all as a comprehensive guidebook for achieving joy and purpose in their endeavours. Finally, my fondest hope is that the book will enrich you with the absolute best of life lessons, without having to learn them painfully through repeated disappointments.

In humble service,

Swami Mukundananda

Section One

....

SPIRITUAL AND EMOTIONAL
WELLNESS

1

Make Friends with Discomfort

Why is progress always so difficult? Because we love to be comfortable. But as the saying goes, 'Growth happens at the end of your comfort zone.' If you wish to improve and evolve, you must develop the ability to handle discomfort. It is the key to growing in life.

Our human nature is the reverse. From infancy, we are taught to hate inconvenience. When we were babies, any expression of uneasiness on our face informed our parents that we were hungry or sleepy, and they promptly responded to alleviate our distress. Now, as grown-ups, on encountering pain, we still bolt in the opposite direction. However, we do not realize that our aversion to discomfort is the leading cause for stagnation.

A psychologist shared with me his experience with treating obesity patients. 'Swamiji, every week I counsel overweight patients whose primary problem is lack of tolerance for pain. The moment they feel the slightest twinge of hunger in their belly, they feel they need to eliminate it by eating.

'The best advice for them is to develop a teeny-weeny tolerance for the stomach's rumblings, but even the thought of it is unacceptable

to them. They have even forgotten what it feels like to be really hungry.'

The psychologist's patients were quick to relieve their discomfort of hunger, but it was not without a cost. They were setting themselves up for suffering the lifelong pain of obesity. Which of these two pains would you prefer?

If the idea of enduring inconvenience for progress is unbearable to you, then please shut this book and visit Netflix instead, where you will get immediate entertainment. For you will not have the capacity to implement the advice in this book. However, if you value 'growth and joy' above 'fun and regret', and are willing to strive for them, then do read on. You will learn tons of invaluable secrets from the *Golden Rules for Living Your Best Life.*

Why tolerating inconvenience is beneficial

- If you dream of mastering the art of public speaking, the only way to overcome the fear of large audiences is to get onto the stage and practise, even though your mind hurts in the process.
- If you wish to become an expert at playing the flute, there is only one known route to mastery. You have to bear the distress of training for it. There is no other way.
- If you aim to become proficient at meditation, it is not going to be easy. The mind will complain in the beginning. You must push past the discomfort, and then the state of naturality will be yours to relish.

The golden rule of life is that achieving growth and positive change is always an uncomfortable process. It requires learning new skills by exerting our mind and intellect beyond their present limits. Despite the unpleasantness, we must continue to practise. Then, the boundaries of our comfort levels expand outwards, and the desired transformation happens. So many things that we do easily now were once difficult for us, but with training, they became natural.

Hence, the secret of success is to not be dissuaded by discomfort. This does not mean that we must deliberately put our hand on the hot stove to create pain. That would be pure stupidity. But we must remember that **the biggest enemy of progress is within us—it is our own inability to cope with inconvenience.**

The mindset of tolerating discomfort

If you abide by the mindset of doing what gives the most pleasure in the moment, you will end up watching movies on TV when you should have been working. You will surf the internet when you should have been exercising. And you will prefer chocolate chip ice cream to healthy salads.

Instead, if you wish for a life of purpose and lasting joy, you must break through the trap of the 'comfort zone'. Living at ease is the biggest hindrance to progress. It prevents you from pushing your boundaries, developing new perspectives and creating new skills.

When you expand your ability to tolerate, you will become unstoppable. You can get up early in the morning, overcome bad habits, save money, lose weight, learn a new language and take online courses, to name just a few. The possibilities are immense.

Let us see how this applies to some of the most basic areas of your life.

Exercise discomfort. We all desire to get into shape. But the dilemma is that a workout involves stretching, exerting and sweating. Undeniably, it is inconvenient and physically uncomfortable. This is why many shy away from it.

However, to develop a shapely body, you must work through that discomfort. Recall the adage: 'No pain, no gain.' It is the only known way to develop endurance and stamina.

Professional discomfort. In the corporate world, there are many who dislike important duties and responsibilities, for they are necessarily difficult. They fear new assignments because of the uncertainty involved. Consequently, they successfully forego discomfort but vegetate in their careers.

However, professional progress entails taking on bigger responsibilities and learning new skills. It may even require jumping into a vocation of which you have no prior experience. So, develop the mindset of embracing the difficult, the inconvenient and the challenging. It is the only way upwards.

Weather discomfort. Hot or cold weather is again not a sign of maha pralaya (end of the world). It is a natural part of the cycle of nature. The Bhagavad Gita states:

> *mātrā-sparśhās tu kaunteya*
> *śhītoṣhṇa-sukha-duḥkha-dāḥ*
> *āgamāpāyino 'nityās*
> *tāṅs-titikṣhasva bhārata*   (2.14)

Lord Krishna explains that the contact between the senses and the sense objects gives rise to fleeting perceptions of happiness and distress. These are non-permanent; they come and go like the winter and summer seasons. One must learn to tolerate them without being disturbed.

Taste discomfort. We all know that a wholesome diet is the key to good health. Then why do we avoid adopting it? The reason is simple. French fries and burgers give momentary pleasure to our taste buds, while health foods are often unpleasant to the tongue.

Imagine, if you could simply train your gustatory sense to accept discomfort. The inconvenience would not mean a personal tragedy, but it would secure your ability to choose whatever foods are best for health.

These are just a few examples to highlight the principle that personality development cannot be accomplished without the willingness to bear pain. Let us now see how we can start living outside our comfort zone, for if we can master this, we can master everything else in life.

Become comfortable with discomfort

Do keep in mind that developing this immensely beneficial personality trait takes time, effort and patience. But, by now, if you have appreciated its importance, then with determination and proper planning, you will surely succeed.

First, you will have to change your attitude towards discomfort. Rather than identifying inconvenience as an enemy, view it as an opportunity for progress; a stepping stone towards awakening your best self.

Second, you will require patience to take small steps, for change always happens slowly. This is the 'One Per Cent Rule'. You cannot go from sinner to saint in a day. Instead, if you keep progressing just a delta of 1 per cent every day, then within a year, you will achieve a transformation of more than 350 per cent!

Third, keep raising the bar and always push a little beyond your limits. If you are too comfortable, then personal growth will not happen. Conversely, if you are too uncomfortable, you will wear yourself out and become discouraged. So, find the golden mean and calibrate your efforts to it.

Finally, aim to reach the stage where bearing beneficial discomfort becomes a joy. Many athletes and peak performers have that attitude. They look forward to experiencing inconvenience, for it indicates progress.

This is the secret to achieving great things. Embrace challenges to become a better version of yourself.

2

Keep a Diary for Self-Improvement

Keeping a daily journal is an intimate way of nurturing and coaching ourselves. In it, we write our dreams, goals, problems, stresses, failures and the record of our life. Soon, it becomes our loyal companion and the bearer of our truths. Not only is it a safe haven for depositing our thoughts, but it is also a way to be accountable to ourselves in our resolves. Our daily appointment with it can be a great way to manage and measure progress in life.

Mahatma Gandhi was fond of maintaining a self-improvement diary. Benjamin Franklin's daily rendezvous with his diary was legendary. He has described his efforts in detail in his famous memoir, *The Autobiography of Benjamin Franklin*. Jagadguru Kripaluji Maharaj also highly recommended introspection with the help of a daily journal.

What to write in the diary? Since our thoughts are intimate and personal, there is no right or wrong content for the diary. It could contain the day's events, creative ideas or notes on personal development. Nevertheless, here are some ideas to use your diary as a spiritual partner.

Put down your self-improvement goals. This could include virtues you wish to develop, weaknesses you want to get rid of and habits you seek to change. You could divide these into the five categories of this book: spirituality, health, relationships, profession and finances.

For example, for your health, you may want to strive towards waking up early, eating a wholesome balanced diet and incorporating an hour of exercise every day. Write these down. Spiritual goals could include the study of sacred texts, overcoming negative traits like envy and developing divine virtues, such as humility and kindness. Again, note down your goals.

When you have your aims spelled out before you and can revisit them regularly, it bestows clarity of thought and a basis for action. Then, on waking up every day, you can systematically choose the items to work upon.

Record your daily progress against your goals. End your day with an assessment of your wins, failures and insights. What goals did you achieve? Feel happy about your progress and resolve to keep up with the thoughts and actions that produced a positive change. Was it enthusiasm or a positive mindset that helped you accomplish your target? If so, maintain those going forward.

Likewise, with care and honesty, evaluate your failures. What prevented you from pursuing or achieving success? Was it laziness, lack of commitment, failure to manage time properly or something else? Document the reasons for your failures. Highlight the learning and then apply the lessons next time around.

List the benefits of the change you wish to accomplish. For example, let us say that you are prone to impatience and intolerance and seek to eliminate these flaws from your personality. This will require a rocksteady resolve and tons of determined effort. So, with the help of your diary, brainstorm the numerous ways in which anger hurts you—the relationships it sours, the frustration it causes, its effect on health, and so on. Similarly, ponder over the gains that would accrue from developing patience—it will free you from agitation and bestow equipoise, among other things. Put them all down.

Once you have the reasons listed in your diary, revisit them daily to refresh the knowledge in your intellect. You will then strengthen your resolve to accomplish the goals and multiply the impetus to your efforts.

Write down gems of wisdom you come across. The process of self-improvement includes expansion of the intellect by acquiring valuable information, reflecting upon it and internalizing it. However, the problem is that the knowledge does not stick. When we learn of useful ideas, say, in a book or from someone, they create an epiphany within us. This is the 'aha moment'. But unfortunately, in a few days, the knowledge slips away and is soon forgotten.

How many wonderful nuggets we have lost in this way? If they all had remained with us, how wise would we be today! That is why it is said: *anabhyāse viṣaṁ vidyā ajīrṇe bhojanaṁ viṣaṁ* 'Just as food eaten when not hungry becomes like poison, similarly, knowledge that is not revised does not benefit.'

Record your worries and problems. Let your diary be a

channel to release stress and anxiety. Rather than thinking about them over and over again, noting them down frees the mind. You can then focus on the present moment. Later, when required, you can analyse your problems with a creative mind. Use your journal to come up with intelligent ideas to handle complex issues.

These are some of the many ideas you can adopt for your journal writing. Do get started on this wonderful tool today itself. If used properly, journaling is an incredible therapeutic source of learning, reflection, accountability and transformation.

3

Gratitude: The Best Attitude

A sense of appreciation for what we have received creates the noble sentiment of gratitude. Psychologists label it as the second-highest positive emotion, after selfless love. Numerous studies have proven that people who are habitually grateful are far happier than those who are not.[1]

What is the attitude of thankfulness? The word 'gratitude' is derived from the Latin word *gratia*, which means 'grateful'. Simply put, **gratitude is the acknowledgement of life's gifts to us.** It is focusing on our blessings rather than our problems. It is the appreciation of the little miracles all around. It is living life with a sense of awe.

Benefits of gratitude. This sublime sentiment plays a key role in the art of positive thinking. Research in the field of positive psychology has linked heightened gratitude to the state of joy. People who practise it also have greater resilience because of their ability to interpret challenging situations positively.

When you genuinely feel thankful from within, you become

---

[1]Brown, Joshua, and Joel Wong, 'How Gratitude Changes You and Your Brain', *Greater Good Magazine*, 6 June 2017, https://bit.ly/3wkH6tL. Accessed on 26 June 2022.

more alive. You are optimistic about the future. Your professional outlook is bright. You can cope better with stress. And you aspire to give back to humanity through service.

Gratitude prevents us from taking things for granted. You may have noticed how you feel when you get a gift, buy a new car or are newly married. There is a sense of excitement and newness. But slowly, it wears off. You start to take these for granted and minimize their importance.

Gratitude changes that. When we appreciate the value of what we have, we are likely to celebrate goodness. So, do not take for granted the gifts you have received from God. These include the earth you walk upon, the air you breathe, the food you eat and the body you inhabit. Feel grateful for them, and your heart will be filled with goodness.

I COUNTED MY BLESSINGS, THEN I
COUNTED EVERYONE ELSE'S BLESSINGS,
AND I'M NOT SO HAPPY ANY MORE!

Gratitude is a transformative emotion. Our brain's neurology is such that harmful feelings and gratefulness cannot coexist. When you are in the appreciative mode, negative emotions will be absent. The more thankful you are, the lower your levels of pessimism and gloom. In fact, studies have shown that being thankful releases serotonin, the 'feel good' neurotransmitter in the brain, which acts as a natural antidepressant.

Why thankfulness does not come naturally. It is the ego within us which is under the illusion that the Universe has been made for fulfilling our puny selfish desires. While the truth is the reverse—we were created to assist in the purpose of the Universe. This false sense of entitlement shows up as excessive complaining, greed and discontentment.

If we can learn to be humble, we will begin to see the Creator's bountiful love for us in the abundance of Creation. Hence, **gratitude is a consequence of humility, which makes us recognize the source of goodness outside of ourselves.**

Note down gratitude. A gratitude journal is a great way of focusing your mind on your blessings. The journal can be a part of the spiritual diary discussed in the previous chapter. Record in it the good that happened to you and the reasons for being thankful. Then, live with those thoughts, and harbour the mindset of gratefulness.

How to practise gratitude. Here are some ways to start implementing it from today.

1. Remember all the basics that you take for granted—like a roof over your head, clean air, good food, and your family

and friends. Every night, before you go to bed, write down about something good that happened in the day, or a good person you met.

2. Learn to see the abundance in nature. Feel the warmth of the sun on a cold winter day. Stop to smell the roses. Feel the coolness of the spring breeze against your skin. The beauty of the blue sky adorned with the fluff of white clouds, and so forth. The perfection in nature is awe-inspiring. Being attentive to small things opens the mind to recognizing the inherent goodness in others as well.

3. Thank God. Humble yourself before your Creator, for He has provided you with everything including your body. Acknowledge His greatness because He is the source of all divinity and goodness.

Thanking God is one of the most powerful of all prayers. It has been highly emphasized in all faiths and religions of the world. In this way, daily celebrate the auspiciousness and abundance that surrounds you, and express your heartfelt appreciation for it to God. **Make gratitude your attitude today, tomorrow and forever!**

4

Do Not Allow Opinions of Others to Define You

We spend too much thought and energy trying to gain the approval of others. While making decisions, 'What will others think' remains a dominant thought in the mind. Instead of running our own race in life, we get bogged down in pleasing others. This must change.

You can never please everyone. No matter what you do, there will always be those who will find fault in you, and discourage and dislike you. That is the nature of worldly people.

Even Mother Sita was not spared of it. Though she had proved her chastity beyond all doubt through a trial by fire, a dhobi (washerman) emerged who cast aspersions on her, and said to his wife, 'I am not like Ram, who brought Sita home after she had stayed in Ravan's Lanka for a year.'

When the Mother of the universe could not be free from detractors in the era of Lord Ram, then it is unrealistic for us to expect everyone's approval in today's environment of hypocrisy. We must wake up to the reality of life. There will always be friends and relatives who belittle us, discredit us and talk negatively of us.

As the expression goes, 'It takes all sorts to make this world.' Some people remain unhappy with you, no matter how nice you are to them. Others just cannot handle your success because it makes them look bad. For their own peace of mind, they love tearing you down.

Therefore, never be surprised if, even after doing good, you still receive caustic censure. If you receive the promotion you deserved, do not expect a standing ovation from everyone around you. Be prepared to hear comments like 'She butters up her boss', 'His rise is all because of office politics', and so on. In fact, the more successful you are, the more criticism will come your way. Do not let the 'gossip police' sabotage your flight to glory.

Remember, it is not about you. People have their own conflicts and emotional issues that need resolution. They carry anger, frustration and disappointment in them. They look for places to dump their baggage. If you allow them, they will empty their garbage onto you. Their negativity is not about you; it is just the way they are. If you consider their approval important, very soon they will start controlling and manipulating you.

The key to handling negativity. Remember this bit of wisdom— **nobody can hurt you unless you allow them to do so.** Here is an anecdote highlighting this principle.

In an institute for the hearing and speech impaired, two inmates had a serious tiff. An official was assigned to straighten out things between them. On reaching their section, the official found one of the men with his back turned to the other, rattling with amusement, while the other was gesturing frantically.

'What is going on here?' said the official, speaking with his hands. 'Why is your partner so annoyed?'

The deaf person gestured with glee, 'We had a fight. Now he wants to swear at me, but I refuse to look in his direction. That is why he is so mad.'

The deaf man was taking advantage of the fact that he could not hear. Hence, the other could only vent fury if he looked towards him. In our case, we will have to learn how to turn a deaf ear to the noise around us.

Deal with it by growing in awareness. When you know someone is differently abled, it evokes your sympathy. Likewise, with a negative person, feel compassion rather than hurt by not taking it personally. One way to do this is to count your blessings and think, 'God is sitting inside the other person too. He is testing my tolerance in an attempt to push me to grow.'

What others say does not define you. People who barely know you feel they have the right to pass judgement upon your worth. Their views are often based on externals and even first impressions. But as the saying goes: 'You cannot judge a book by its cover.' Factually, what others say characterizes them, not you.

Do also bear in mind that all the praise we receive will come to naught upon death. We leave it all behind and move on to the afterlife. At that time, the only thing of importance will be the extent to which God was pleased by our life and works. **So, rather than trying to be *called good*, focus on *becoming good* in the eyes of the Lord, Who is the constant witness to your karmas.**

5

Grow in the Face of Adversity

Like the changing seasons, our lives go through many cycles of favourable and unfavourable times. Dualities are a part of the world. There is heat and cold, night and day, happiness and distress. We must be prepared for both. In fact, in this world of maya (God's material energy), reversals are more prevalent than victories. Therefore, your **success in life depends on how effectively you deal with adversity.**

It is so easy to feel hopeless, fearful and anxious in the face of adversities. These negative emotions can consume us if we are not careful. However, with awareness and practise, we can learn to respond differently. Then, we will not only handle challenges with poise but also turn them to our advantage. People who cross over to the other side of challenging times find that the journey made them grow from within.

Let me narrate the inspiring story of Kalpana Saroj. Hers is a story of inner strength, conviction and triumph over hardships. Born in the lower strata of a Dalit community, Kalpana faced numerous challenges. Married off at the age of 12, she practically served as a maid in her husband's family, looking after the basic needs of 10 members. Often abused and beaten, she was neglected and in a decrepit state.

Her father later rescued her and took her home. However, her community ostracized her for returning home after marriage. Devastated, Kalpana attempted suicide by drinking insecticide.

Fortunately, she survived. This became a turning point in her life. With a resolve to succeed, she travelled to Mumbai and started working in a garment factory as a tailor. That made her self-reliant, and after her father lost his job, she invited her family to live with her, as she remained the only breadwinner amongst them. During this time, her sister fell ill, and they didn't have money for her treatment. 'Please save me,' were her sister's last words. These words left a mark on Kalpana's heart, and she decided to never let that happen again. She realized the importance of money.

Subsequently, Kalpana utilized a government loan scheme and procured a loan of ₹50,000. She started her own tailoring business. With a second loan, while honing her entrepreneurial skills, she began creating high-end furniture at economical prices.

By now, she was a famous and powerful businesswoman. Upon the request of desperate workers at Kamani Tubes, the metal company under dire debt, she took over as the Chief Executive Officer (CEO) of the corporation. Yet another turning point for Kalpana! She managed to pay back all the debts and steered the company to prosperity—today having an estimated turnover of ₹2,000 crore annually.

This real-life story of Kalpana Saroj is a blazing example of fortitude and perseverance in the face of adversity. She converted every hardship into an opportunity for learning and self-growth. Instead of succumbing to hopelessness, she lifted herself higher by responding with the will to succeed. This ability to approach life's challenges positively helps unleash our infinite potential.

At times, suffering comes directly from God. Sometimes deprivations are deliberately sent to us by the Lord Himself, to arrange for our spiritual elevation. The Shreemad Bhagavatam states:

> *tam bhraṅśhayāmi sampadbhyo*
> *yasya chechchāmyanugraham* (10.27.16)

In this verse, Lord Krishna says that when He wishes to bestow His highest treasures upon someone, He first prepares that person by giving suffering.

When a child is engrossed in a toy and has forgotten its mother, she gets her servant to snatch it away. The child cries initially, but then remembers its mother and cries out for her. The mother comes and feeds her baby.

On seeing the toy snatched away, one could have wrongly concluded that the mother is being cruel. However, it was also a manifestation of her maternal affection.

When facing hardships, think: 'lessons learned', not 'loss'. If your goal is worldly comfort and gratification, then material suffering is certainly a bad thing. But if you seek spiritual progress, then adversity provides the opportunity to evolve and become a better version of yourself.

The challenges we face in adversities force us to search for answers. When we exert ourselves, we find the wisdom to handle situations and develop virtues of moral strength, resilience and forbearance. This is how we grow in the face of difficulties. To learn more about cultivating a positive mindset and growing in the face of challenges, read my book, *7 Mindsets for Success, Happiness and Fulfilment.*

6

Harness the Power of Self-Talk

All that we are is the result of what we have thought.
—Gautam Buddha

Have you wondered the reason for the variety in human attitudes? Some people have the heart of a lion, while others are bound by a series of fears. Some are full of zeal, though others are hopelessly pessimistic. Some are lazy and careless, and some are steadfastly disciplined.

These diverse perspectives can be traced back to our self-talk—what we say to ourselves, within our mind. Someone keeps repeating inwardly, 'I am healthy and well.' Another's mental chatter is, 'I am miserable and sick.' Though it may seem trivial, this inner dialogue forges the attitudes that make our personality.

Self-talk programmes the subconscious. Our subconscious mind, which is a repository of impressions and memories, does not differentiate between right and wrong, or true and false. It simply believes whatever we feed it through the conscious mind. Hence, we can programme it with positivity, hope and faith. On the flip side, we can just as easily condition it with cynicism, doubt and fear.

Once programmed, the subconscious begins to supply thoughts to our conscious mind, as per its conditioning. These manifest in the form of our mindsets, beliefs and biases. If the self-talk happened to be destructive, the subconscious becomes our own worst enemy. It then sabotages us with limiting perspectives, phobias and self-doubt. But the reverse is also true.

Through our inner dialogue, we can programme our psyche with success stories of valour, altruism and achievement. The most decorated Olympian of all time, Michael Phelps, writes in his book, *No Limits: The Will to Succeed*, 'If you say "can't" you're restricting what you can do or ever will do.'[2]

Here are a few effective ways of indulging in positive self-talk.

Become aware of your inner chatter. Start listening to the thoughts you often repeat to yourself. Are you overcritical of yourself? Are you supportive and encouraging? How do you respond to problems? Be honest about whether your self-talk is negative or positive. Recognize any toxic dialogues and write them down.

Stop and replace negative self-talk. The good news is that our brain is extremely malleable. It can be reframed to leave aside old patterns of thought and adopt new ones. Use this to your benefit.

- Instead of saying, 'I won't be able to lose weight', tell yourself, 'I will eat healthy and reach my goal with exercise and diet control'.

---

[2]Phelps, Michael, *No Limits: The Will to Succeed*, Free Press, 2009, Kindle ebook.

- Instead of cribbing, 'I'm terrible, I'll fail at my interview', think, 'I will prepare properly for the job interview, and all will go well'.
- Replace thoughts of lethargy by saying you have plenty of energy and enthusiasm.

In this way, substitute harmful musings with optimistic dialogues. Do this until it becomes habitual.

Use positive self-talk daily. Internal messages of hope, faith and courage are referred to as positive affirmations. When they are iterated mentally, they go deep within to change our attitude, beliefs and actions. Some examples are:

- *'I'm grateful for my life and the abundant blessings of God.'*
- *'The Universe is on my side; good things happen to me.'*
- *'I am close to achieving my goal. I will not give up; I can do it.'*
- *'I see the positive side of things and remain calm in adverse situations.'*

Empowering affirmations hardwire our subconscious. These then become a part of our psyche, and we develop life-transforming attitudes.

Watch your choice of words—there is tremendous power in them. Your choice of phrases is more important than you think. Language that is drastic is often extreme and evokes similar emotions within. Some of the worst kind of self-talk is: 'I can never learn to sing', 'I am clumsy and always dropping things', and so on. Hence, in your inner dialogue, eliminate words such as 'cannot' and 'never'. Very few things in life are final.

In conclusion, take control of your self-talk. Delete the chatter that does not belong. Embrace that which uplifts, builds and sustains. In this way, programme your subliminal mind to be the engine that steers your life towards success. For more detail on the subconscious, you can refer to my book, *The Science of Mind Management*.

7

Do a Social Media Detox

Do you check your messages as soon as you wake up in the morning and keep the phone with you when you go to bed? Is the urge to take your phone to the bathroom irresistible? Do you find it easier to leave a comment on social media than converse with people in the real world? During social functions, are you busy clicking pics and posting them on Facebook and Instagram?

If you nodded affirmatively to any of the above, then you have lost control over your life due to social media addiction. You need to stop sharing everything with virtual friends on your social network. Instead, connect with friends and family in person. You might say, 'But why should I do that? I enjoy it.' Let us understand why.

Social platforms laid bare. Many people on social media try to portray themselves as having a perfect life. They flaunt their well-toned physique, swanky cars, huge homes, stories of travel and success. However, they omit to post about their emotional distresses and behavioural addictions.

Invariably, social media influencers use smart lighting or Photoshop to create a façade of happiness. They seek 'likes' and 'comments' as a form of validation. Innocent people look at these and form an inferiority complex, believing that their own life is less successful with not as much 'happening'. As a result, the lure of surfing on social media makes them miserable.

Cyberbullying is a major menace. On social media, people can be cruel for no reason. This distresses several teens and adults, even driving some to suicide. Several studies have shown that excessive use of technology can cause mental disorders, strain relationships and affect well-being. The irony is that without your knowing, you get adversely affected.

'But how can I live without being connected to social media in this age?' you may ask. 'I will miss out on important activities.'

Do not worry. This chapter does not tell you to give up your gadgets and delete your social media accounts. It only teaches the right way to use them, for your benefit, rather than as a detriment. However, before working on any solution, it is necessary to understand the problem in detail.

Track your 'online' time. First, track the time you spend on your phone for about a week. Several apps can help you do this. The figures may surprise you, as people often underestimate the time they remain hooked to their mobiles. Now, let us move to the solution.

Reduce social media time at home. First, cut down the time you spend on digital gadgets at home. After work or college or on the weekends, conscientiously keep your phone at a designated place and do not carry it with you. If you must check your phone, go to that place, see the specific mail that you are expecting or attend the call, and then leave the phone there itself.

After a few days, when you are comfortable with this new schedule of using your phone, you can go a step further and stop all the sound notifications for the social media apps. The next step would be to disable all social media apps that are not necessary and check them only on a desktop or laptop.

Initially, you may feel you are missing out by not being connected to the world. But do not worry; instead, use that time to connect with the world nearby or inside you. Play with your child, help your spouse with chores, reignite the habit of reading or go out for a walk. Slowly, you will find that it is much more enjoyable and productive to spend time with your family. Alternatively, you could focus on your hobby. In this way, use your time wisely.

Do not take gadgets to bed. Next, the phone, tablet or laptop should not go to bed with you. Keep the gadgets outside the room. Use bedtime to unwind and relax the mind in preparation for a restful sleep. Instead of scrolling through the internet, you can introspect, contemplate and meditate. In fact, to best utilize this time, absorb yourself in remembrance of God. Sing His glories and chant His name. These few steps should help you save substantial time and reduce your stress, anxiety and insomnia.

Wake up 'offline'. Again, in the morning, resist checking Facebook or other social media channels. Waking up to notifications, missed messages and emails floods our mind with information and pulls down the consciousness. Since your mind is fresh in the morning, this time can be better utilized for meaningful work, exercising, prioritizing the day and for your daily sadhana. Consider switching on the phone after your morning routine has been completed.

Minimize the use of social media at work. If you cut off unwanted social media apps in the office, you will improve productivity, complete work on time and leave the office early. Who does not want to do that?

Develop a habit of quickly skimming through your messages in not more than 15 minutes before or after lunch. Make it a point to relish the food and enjoy the company at lunch, rather than be on your phone. This will help you connect better with your colleagues and be more effective at work.

For the first few days, you will feel the urge to look at your mobile or connect to certain sites from the laptop, but with a firm resolve, you can quickly get over it. The subject of staying focused is very important in today's world. Hence, I have elaborated it further in the chapter, 'Stay Focused in a Distracted World'.

When used with self-discipline, social media can be a good avenue to enhance our knowledge, interact with like-minded people and connect globally. However, we have to be mindful to use it wisely and not become its slave.

8

Understand and Overcome Fear

We all can attest to feeling scared at one time or another in life. This could have been due to simple things: a needle at the doctor's office, failing in an exam, public speaking or a dreadful interview. It could also have presented itself as uncertainty of the future, apprehension of rejection, and the like. Since fear is so prevalent, this chapter is dedicated to helping you understand it and deal with it effectively.

What is fear? It is an alarming reaction to something that threatens our safety. We are genetically wired with it. Fear's primary role is 1) to keep us safe, and 2) to mobilize us in coping with potential danger.

The problem arises when it is irrational and disproportionate to the actual danger. Such fear is called 'phobia'. In modern times, imminent dangers to life are few, but people blow them up in their mind, such as fear of heights, fear of medical procedures, fear of insects and fear of poverty. What triggers such irrational fear, and how it can be overcome?

Causes of fear. All organisms in nature instinctively act to preserve themselves. We humans are no exception. We possess innate protective responses to external threats. Fear is the emotional stimulus that triggers them.

For example, if someone were to attack us with a bat, we would instantly and instinctively move out of the way. If a wolf were to appear before us, we would quickly respond by giving fight or taking flight. Such instinctive fears are not wrong—they are essential to our self-preservation.

Other fears develop as a result of a frightening experience. Let us say, someone fell into a pond as a child; subsequently, she developed a fear for all water bodies. This explains why some people are hydrophobic, claustrophobic, agoraphobic, and so on. Such phobias could even develop from watching frightening things happen to others. When they get bloated out of proportion in our mind, they create irrational dreads that cripple our ability to function effectively.

Having understood the causes of fear, let us now delve into some simple techniques to overcome them.

Understand fear. The first step is to see fear for what it is—yet another emotion created by the mind. Though it may seem very real and unmanageable, like every other emotion the mind generates, fear can be controlled.

Bridle your overactive imagination. Michel de Montaigne, the French philosopher, said: 'My life has been filled with terrible misfortune; most of which never happened.' Studies have corroborated that 91 per cent of our worries are false alarms and never materialize.[3] They are a result of negative thought

---

[3]Gillihan, Seth J., 'How Often Do Your Worries Actually Come True?' *Psychology Today*, 19 July 2019, https://bit.ly/3O1EyGV. Accessed on 26 June 2022.

processes, and for no logical reason, we seem to imagine the most terrible outcomes.

For example, suppose your child is late from school one day. Your mind immediately fabricates horror stories. Maybe the child is lost, kidnapped or ill. Without knowing the facts, you allow your thoughts to run wild. This is referred to as 'catastrophic thinking'.

The way to overcome this tendency is not to jump to conclusions without all the facts. Instead, question fearful thoughts when the mind generates them. Do this by pausing and becoming aware of your thoughts and then consciously weeding out the irrational ones.

Examine the worst-case scenario. One powerful technique of eliminating dread is by exploring the worst possible outcome. Is it really as awful as your mind has convinced you to believe?

For example, you may fear upsetting your boss and getting fired. The worst outcome in this situation may be that you lose your job. In which case, you may endure some hardship financially, but at the same time, you may land a better job or use that opportunity to start a new career or business.

What seems as really terrible, or the worst, is often not so. Rather, many seemingly awful events actually end up benefiting us in one way or another.

Focus on your efforts, not the results. Fear of possible negative outcomes to our actions can keep us from many achievements. For instance, some students never ask any questions in class due to fear of judgement. They are willing to accept a lower grade as a result. People-pleasers, who cannot say 'No', fear rejection. Likewise, some are afraid of ruin or failure, which prevents them from taking risks in life.

Stay in the present. In all these cases, you fear the potential negative results of your actions. And that does not help. It shifts your focus into the future. 'If the worst happens, then what?', 'If my fears come true, then what?' However, any work can only be done properly when we pay our full attention to it. In this scenario, irrational fear distracts focus and saps the thought energy.

The way out is to shift attention to your efforts. Ultimately, the only thing in our hands is the effort. Attending to it to the best of our abilities is the most effective way of avoiding what you fear may happen.

Improve your skill set. Expertise helps overcome fear because it improves your confidence level. If you have practised the subject well, you will not fear delivering a lecture on it, as much as you would if you were clueless about the matter. Hence, growing in knowledge and skills is a powerful antidote to fear. It not only improves your abilities but also prepares you to better handle intimidating conditions.

Expose yourself to the object of your fear. Psychologists talk of the phenomenon of 'habituation'. It refers to our decreasing nervous response on repeated exposure to something. This could seem counterintuitive. Most people attempt to cope with anxiety by avoiding the situation that prompts it. However, avoidance prevents the nervous system from habituating. The feared situation remains new, which perpetuates the fear.

Instead, we must learn to face our fears and claim back the power they have over us. When you pick up the courage to do the things that frighten you, their dread will dissolve. And the more you repeatedly practise being in uncomfortable situations, the more you will conquer your fears.

Overcome attachment. Ultimately, the root cause of all fear is attachment. This is just as fever is the symptom when one has malaria. Now, if we were to treat the fever, while ignoring the malaria, it would not work. Likewise, fear is the warning sign, while the disease within is excessive clinging to something.

Detachment, on the other hand, enables us to accept lack of bodily comfort and security. Sage Bhartrihari explains:

> bhoge roga bhayaṁ kule chyuti bhayaṁ
>   vitte nṛipālād bhayaṁ
> sarvaṁ vastu bhayāvahaṁ
>   bhuvi nṛiṇāṁ vairāgyamevābhayaṁ

'Attachment to sensual pleasures results in fear of disease; clinging to high position causes fear of downfall; affection for wealth results in fear of poverty. Any excessive attachment creates fear. While detachment immediately bestows freedom from fear.'

The fear of death is considered the biggest fear in people's minds. Its cause is, again, attachment. The Sanskrit term for it is *abhiniveśh,* which literally means 'clinging to the things around us'. Thus, the prime remedy for any fear is to rid the mind of all attachments.

9

Nurture Your Spirituality

What is the importance of spirituality, and what is the benefit of cultivating it in life? In this age of science, we grow up learning a very reductionist world view in school and college. We are taught that all life is just a combination of atoms and molecules, and the world was created by an accidental 'Big Bang'. The problem with this perspective is that it misses out on so many intrinsic human needs. The chief amongst these is spirituality.

What is spirituality? It is a belief in the existence of something sacred and divine, beyond the mundane objects around us. It is an appreciation of our soul nature, distinct from the material body. Spirituality is behaving in alignment with our higher-self. It is a connection with something bigger than us; it is the search for a deeper meaning in life.

In the Hindu tradition, and around the world, spirituality is practised in a variety of ways. Whatever bona fide way you adopt for yourself, it bestows benefits that are indispensable for your well-being. Here are some important ones.

Spirituality helps develop good values and beliefs. As we go through life, we are presented with numerous options and are required to make choices.

- In this ethical dilemma, what is my duty?
- In the present situation, what should I prioritize and why?
- What should I make as the goal of my life?

If we do not have a system of beliefs to reference, making these choices can become overwhelming and impossible. Sacred books of spirituality offer divine wisdom for our personal structure of beliefs. They reveal the values that great saints successfully practised. Thus, they clarify our path for moving ahead in life.

Spirituality helps us see the big picture. The demands of our daily routines entangle us in mundane tasks. We are obliged to run from morning till night to earn money. We are required to take care of our family. But while fulfilling these worldly necessities, we also have a need for a higher fulfilment, beyond the mundane. Spiritual wisdom helps us connect with elevated ideas and noble concepts.

Spirituality nurtures our connection with Creation. As children, we had a very 'I'-centred world view. Life was all about *our* desires, aspirations and fears. The immense materialism of modern society reinforced that world view. It made us believe success in life was all about personal fame, wealth and comfort. However, as we grow spiritually and raise our spiritual awareness, we begin to appreciate the interrelatedness of all life. Then, we develop a healthy attitude towards all creatures and the entire Universe.

Spirituality helps us become a better person. Deep within, we all aspire to become a better version of ourselves. Yet, self-transformation does not come easy. We struggle with negative thoughts and detrimental habits. In this situation, a good spiritual belief system hands us the tools and practices required for improving ourselves. It also strengthens our commitment to practising self-discipline in life. Consequently, our journey of inner purification speeds up.

It is a pity that despite all these benefits, spiritual knowledge is often looked down upon in academic circles. To talk about the soul and God in corporate boardroom discussions or scientific interactions is considered old-fashioned. In India, in the name of secularism, spirituality has been eliminated from education. As a result, you go through your entire school and college life without any reference to spirituality.

Do not let pseudo-intellectual propaganda sway you. In fact, spirituality is like the 'one', while everything else is like 'zeros'. With 'one' in the lead, every 'zero' behind it adds value, but without it, life remains zero—futile and purposeless. So, do prioritize your devotion and nurture it with dedication. The remaining articles in this spirituality section of the *Golden Rules for Living Your Best Life* provide you with invaluable wisdom for your spiritual practice.

10

Find Your Purpose in Life

Your life's purpose is the central motivating goal of your existence. It is the reason why you do anything at all—eat, breathe, earn, learn and work. Knowing it has a transformational effect on your life.

If you wake up every morning, excited at yet another day to live and work meaningfully, it means you have found a glorious purpose. However, if your first act in the morning is to find entertainment on social media and TV, it is a sign that you have not yet discovered your aim in the world. In that case, you would do well to take inspiration from the famous words of Martin Luther King Jr: 'If you haven't found something you are willing to die for, you aren't fit to live.'

Let us see some of the benefits that accrue from a well-defined life goal.

Living with purpose enriches the quality of life. Success in our endeavours requires energetic and passionate effort. Thus, enthusiasm is a key ingredient for enriched living. What, then, is the best way to inspire ourselves and retain that motivation at all times?

This is an important question. It is often put to me when I

visit college campuses. Students say, 'Swamiji, when we hear motivational speakers, we become inspired. But three days later, we discover the inspiration has disappeared, and we again feel listless. Is there any method for sustaining our motivation?'

This is where knowledge of our life purpose makes a difference. **Nothing provides deeper and more lasting inspiration than a powerful cause that we passionately believe in. It leads to a sense of higher duty, which ignites us with the enthusiasm to do our best every day.**

People even live healthier and longer when they believe their life serves a greater good. This was revealed by the Blue Zones Study done on Okinawa centenarians in Japan. Researchers noticed that senior Okinawans were convinced they were leading a life of purpose, even at the age of 100.[4] They were clear about their roles and responsibilities in society and could readily articulate the reason for getting up in the morning.

'That is all very well,' you may say. 'But how do I discover my purpose in life?' Here are some helpful ways.

Awaken your curiosity. Do not be like the person who was so busy running that he did not even stop to think where and why he was going. Instead, take a pause to ponder over the fundamental questions of life.

- Who am I?
- Why did I come into this world?
- How did the world come into being?

---

[4]García, Héctor, and Francesc Miralles, *Ikigai: The Japanese Secret to a Long and Happy Life*, Penguin Group (USA) LLC, August 2017, Kindle ebook.

– Having come to this planet, what is my duty in life?

Finding answers to these questions is the very reason we have received the human form. The *Hitopadesh* states:

> *āhāra-nidrā-bhaya-maithunaṁ cha*
> *sāmānyam etat paśhubhir narāṇām*
> *jñānaṁ hi teṣhām adhiko viśheṣho*
> *jñānena hīnāḥ paśhubhiḥ samānāḥ*

'Even animals engage in bodily activities like eating, sleeping, defending and mating. The speciality of the human form is the opportunity to enquire into the meaning of life itself. Without such a quest for the Truth, what difference remains between the animals and us?'

This also requires you to keep an open mind. The purpose of your life could very well turn out to be something that you rejected in your younger years or an alternative path for which you might not get familial support.

Let hurts and wounds provoke curiosity. Very often, negative experiences provide the impetus to introspect and search for satisfactory answers. Usually, this search for proper knowledge leads us out of our comfort zone; we tend to turn to spiritual wisdom to seek comfort and solace. Innumerable sages in history were pushed by personal hurts to set out on a spiritual quest. Sometimes, the sufferings of others were the spark that ignited their quest.

The story of the Buddha is world famous. As Siddharth, he was a prince and had all the luxuries and comforts anyone could hope for. But on a tour of his kingdom, for the first time in his life, he saw a sick person, an old man and a corpse. Witnessing this suffering provoked him to ponder over the nature of life and that set him on the path to enlightenment.

Develop the habit of reading. Good books seed our intellect with wisdom. They widen the scope of our thinking and make us better informed. Reading is particularly beneficial for the youth, who are consciously enquiring into and determining their life goals. At this stage, even good works of fiction help them get experiences of the personalities in the novel. They get to read about varieties of life purposes and broaden their vision to decide their own goals.

Delve into sacred scriptures and associate with holy personalities. The Vedic texts and holy saints are an unparalleled source of wisdom on the subject of life goals. They are the specialists on the questions: 1) Who are we? 2) What should be the aim of our life? 3) How can we attain our supreme goal?

Sometimes, the search for our purpose can become elusive. If wrongly defined, we can short-change ourselves by aligning with trivial or even meaningless goals. Hence, for the sake of completion of the topic, below is a simplified explanation of the universal life goals.

Our highest purpose in the human form is to complete the evolutionary journey of our soul, by achieving the supreme perfectional state. In simple words, we must strive to be the best that we can be.

The second goal is to manifest our potential talents for the pleasure of the Lord, and as a result, make a difference through the work we do. Simply put, this means to do the best that we can do. Then what happens?

When we go to sleep each day knowing that we tried our best, it gives us deep satisfaction, and we begin to feel the best that we can feel. In this way, **the purpose of our life is to be good, to do good and to feel good.**

11

Look for Happiness in the Right Places

*J*ustin Bieber is one of the world's most popular music artists in
the last 15 years. He is a Grammy award winner, and his albums
have sold over 150 million copies. At the time of writing this book,
he was the second-most followed person on Twitter worldwide.
Yet, during an interview on NME.com, he opened up about his
miseries, '... I'm struggling just to get through the days. ... You get
lonely... People see the glam and the amazing stuff, but they don't
know the other side. This life can rip you apart.'[5]

Is Justin Bieber the only celebrity to express melancholy? Not at
all. There is an unending list of cine stars, athletes, TV artistes
and royalty who have publicly revealed their sentiments of
despair, hollowness, panic and even depression.

Prince Harry said in an interview with The Telegraph *a couple
of years ago, '... I have spent most of my life saying, "I'm fine"... I
can safely say that losing my mum at the age of 12, and therefore
shutting down all of my emotions for the last 20 years has had
quite a serious effect on not only my personal life but my work as*

---

[5]Flood, Alex, 'Justin Bieber releases new videos for every track on "Purpose"',
nme.com, 15 November 2015, https://bit.ly/3CncoUx. Accessed on 26 June
2022.

well ... I have probably been very close to a complete breakdown on numerous occasions...[6]

These are just a couple of examples of people who possess riches, fame, adulation and opulence. Apparently, they 'have it all'. Yet, despite the superstar status and smiling faces on social media, true joy remains a distant dream. The external façade is deceiving, for internally they are miserable.

Ultimately, the bottom line is that we all want happiness. If we do not get it, then naturally, even the biggest success seems purposeless and unfulfilling.

The importance of happiness. Is it possible to just step out of this mad chase for joy, and instead, look for something else? That option is not available. The longing for happiness comes from God Himself. He is an ocean of bliss. And as His little parts, we naturally seek bliss. Hence, **the yearning for happiness is as natural to our being as wetness is to water and heat is to fire. It can never be quelled. The only option we have is to look for it in the wrong place or the right one.**

The search for fulfilment. When the quest for happiness is the universal common desire of all, then why are so few finding it? The answer is that people are looking for it in the wrong places. How ludicrous is it that we madly pursue happiness but have no clear idea where to find it?

Where, then, is the bliss we are searching for? And where is

---

[6]Gordon, Bryony, 'What Really Happened When Prince Harry Opened Up to Bryony Gordon about his Mental Health', *telegraph.co.uk*, 17 May 2018, https://bit.ly/3Cns6Pq. Accessed on 26 June 2022.

it not? Where will our search be an exercise in futility? And where will it be worthwhile? To understand the answers to these questions, know that there are primarily four categories of happiness you can savour. These are:

1. **From tamasic entities and pursuits**, such as intoxicants, meat-eating, gambling, sleeping and anger. Pursuing this kind of happiness plunges our soul into the darkness of ignorance.

2. **From rajasic entities and pursuits.** This is the pleasure we get by indulging our senses in the objects of their gratification. The problem is that there is no satiation. You can compare it to an itch. It is tempting to scratch, but that does not solve the problem; the itch comes back again. The desires of the senses are just the same. Fulfilling them never satiates; on the contrary, they get inflamed even further.

3. **From sattvic entities and pursuits**, such as knowledge, stillness of mind and philanthropy. This kind of pleasure illumines us, nurtures good virtues and elevates our consciousness. Yet, even sattvic happiness cannot satisfy us because it is material, while our soul is divine.

4. **Divine bliss.** Unlike the previous three, this is happiness that does not fade with time. Not only does it stay ever fresh, but it also keeps increasing. The *Chhāndogya Upanishad* states: *yo vai bhumā tatsukham* (7.23.1) 'Divine bliss is infinite in extent.'

In conclusion, if we wish to be infinitely happy forever, then we must make divine bliss our goal. How can we do that? For it, we will first need to give up a mental disease. Let us learn about it next.

The destination disease. Most people realize they are presently unhappy, but they expect that on reaching a future goal, they will surely become joyous. Here are some examples of the destination disease:

- *'I have ₹10 lakh today; when I get ₹1 crore, then I will surely have it all and that will make me happy.'*
- *'I am junior clerk today; when I become head clerk, I can direct others and that will make me happy.'*
- *'I live in a one-bedroom apartment; when I get a three-bedroom bungalow, I will feel secure and happy.'*

We all think that a higher standard of living must result in more happiness. The problem is that on reaching the higher standard, we find it does not satisfy. So, we now plan for more luxuries, greater wealth and higher positions. In the meantime, every day passes by in drudgery. It is like the veritable 'mirage in the desert' that keeps fading away as we move towards it.

The illusion of future happiness creates the destination disease. It makes us think, 'I can afford to feel wretched today, because I am hopeful that tomorrow will bring me joy.' Instead, we must figure out how to make the present moment blissful, not the final station alone.

True happiness is within. Ironically, to be happy we need neither luxuries, nor high positions, nor big bank balances. Saint Kabir put it so powerfully: *pānī bīch mīn piyāsī, mohi suni suni āvat hāṁsī* 'If a fish in the water were to complain of thirst, how ludicrous it would seem!' Likewise, the ocean of happiness, God, is sitting within each of us. All that is required is to cleanse our mind and bring our consciousness closer to

Him. Then we will experience His infinite bliss and become completely satisfied.

Thus, the real way to be happy is to go within yourself—to become a better person. Simple, isn't it! For that, we must utilize the tools and techniques for inner upliftment presented in this rule book. As our mind and intellect get purified by engaging in loving devotion to God and becoming how He wishes us to become, we will find the floodgates of happiness opening up from within. And then, we will become genuinely happy!

12

Practise Humility: The King of Virtues

Study the lives of the icons of history, and you will find a common virtue amongst them—they were all exceptionally modest. Here is what some of them had to say:

I was like a child playing on the seashore, while the whole undiscovered ocean lay in front of me.
        —Isaac Newton, the greatest scientist in history

The only true wisdom is in knowing you know nothing.
        —Socrates, the wise old man of Greece

We come nearest to the great when we are great in humility.
                        —Rabindranath Tagore,
                        India's first Nobel prize winner

God hates pride and loves humbleness.
        —Sage Narad in his *Bhakti Darshan*

Since the books of wisdom and the great luminaries both emphasized unpretentiousness, let us take a look at some of its benefits.

Humbleness makes us aware of our defects. We all have numerous shortcomings because we have been in the world of maya since endless lifetimes. However, the biggest amongst these is pride. It makes us blind to our faults, and thereby hinders our future growth. A proud person thinks, 'I am okay. There is no need for me to improve.'

In contrast, humility gets us to cognize our weaknesses, which is the first step in the journey of life transformation.

Humble people are eager to learn. Proud people are not teachable. Either they do not feel the need to learn from others, or they are too haughty to request for knowledge. On the other hand, modest people realize that they do not know everything. They ask questions, invite feedback and listen with an open mind. Then, they apply those learnings to develop their personality.

Hence, the sign of true knowledge is not pride; it is humility. The *Hitopadesh* states: *vidyā dadāti vinayaṁ* 'True education leads to humbleness.'

Humility makes us grateful. When we realize we are not entitled to abundance, then we become appreciative and thankful for what we have received. Consider this conversation I had with a humble man.

I once asked someone, 'How are you?'

He said, 'I am much better than I deserve to be.'

His answer expressed the spirit of humbleness so wonderfully!

The secret of this man's positive mindset was his lack of pride. Compare it with the attitude of the haughty who take all their blessings as entitlements. In addition, they have a list of complaints about things that they did not receive.

Humbleness opens our eyes to the glory of God. In every speck of creation—from the tiniest quarks to the largest galaxies—the wondrous miracle of God manifests itself. Then, what blinds people from accepting the existence of the Creator? It is their unrelenting ego that elevates the 'self' over God. As Rumi, the great thirteenth-century Persian poet, said: 'The Ego is a veil between humans and God.'

The ego is unwilling to accept an inferior position. It feels affronted on nurturing sentiments of reverence and devotion. Chaitanya Mahaprabhu emphasized humility as the very foundation of spiritual practice:

tṛiṇād api sunīchena, taror api sahiṣhṇunā
amāninā mānadena, kīrtanīyaḥ sadā hariḥ

(Shikshashtakam verse 3)

'Be humbler than a blade of grass and more tolerant than a tree. Do not desire any respect for yourself, while giving all respect to others. In this state of mind, always chant the Names of God.'

Having discussed the benefits of humility, let us see how we can train ourselves in this foremost of virtues.

Stop bragging. Everyone realizes how distasteful it is to blow one's own trumpet, except for the one who indulges in it. The irony is that we engage in self-aggrandizement thinking it will impress people, but it results in the reverse—it awakens their envy. On the other hand, when we take the humble position, it evokes compassion and kindness in others.

When you are wrong, admit it. The only person who never makes mistakes is God. Everyone else is human and will often trip up. If you try to cover it up with an air of invincibility, you will lose the trust and respect of others. It will also create a hollowness in your character, for in your heart, you will be aware of your shortcomings and feel like a hypocrite.

Instead, if you admit your lapses, you will develop genuineness in your personality. Believe me, others will not hate you for it, rather, they will be more sympathetic and will open up to you.

Contemplate on the greatness of God. A mountain appears to be as tall as us when we are 500 miles away from it. But as we move closer, we realize our tininess in comparison. Similarly, in forgetfulness of the Supreme, we could suffer from delusions of grandeur, and think, 'I really am something.' But when we compare ourselves with His magnificence, we become naturally humble.

Attribute your accomplishments to His grace. This is the nature and spirit of devotion. Take inspiration from the saints. When they notice good in themselves, they credit it to God's causeless grace. And when they realize their shortcomings, they think, 'I am not surrendered; that is why I failed to attract divine grace.'

Finally, what should we do if, having realized the importance of humbleness and endeavoured to develop it, we still find mounds of pride within ourselves? Jagadguru Kripaluji Maharaj recommended: 'Pray to the Lord Himself to bestow true humility upon us.'

13

Choose Your Beliefs Well

Your beliefs are an enormously powerful force in your life. They determine how you perceive situations and events. Beliefs shape your thoughts and emotions. And for better or for worse, your choices and actions get aligned with them. While good beliefs can lift you to incredible heights, poor beliefs can hurt you like nothing else.

Beliefs define the reality in which we live. If we are convinced that people are intrinsically bad, we will nurture matching emotions. Consequently, hatred and suspicion will dominate our thoughts, and even the best intended gestures of people will seem malicious to us.

The truth may be quite different. We may actually be interacting with excellent people. However, our experience of them will get moulded by our convictions. In this manner, what we passionately believe in becomes the reality of our life.

Nobody is devoid of beliefs. The idea that only religious people have faith is very wrong. Atheists swear that the world was created by itself, even though they were not present when it happened. Likewise, theists are absolutely convinced about the existence of God, even though they have not yet seen Him. This goes to show that we all have faith, and we live by it, although we may have no evidence to back it up.

Without beliefs, we cannot survive in this world. Consider a simple example of the need for faith. You visit a doctor whose name you cannot pronounce. He writes a prescription that you are unable to read. You carry it to a pharmacist whose face you have never seen before. He hands you a medicine with ingredients you know nothing about. Yet, you consume it and get cured.

The conclusion is that we all possess faith. The choice before us is where to place it.

Beliefs define our potential. They create in us a feeling of certainty about things. For example, if you utterly believe that you have the potential to succeed in life, you will persist no matter what happens. You will literally be unstoppable. Conversely, if you believe that success is all a matter of having connections at the right places—and you do not have them—you will easily get discouraged whenever the going gets tough.

This is the principle behind the rich dad/poor dad theory.

A child born in poverty grows up with the conditioning, 'For me, life is supposed to be penurious. I cannot do much to cast away my poverty.'

In contrast, a child born in a wealthy home develops a different conditioning, 'Even if losses impoverish me, they will only be temporary. I am meant to live in luxury, and I am confident I can very quickly become rich again.'

In both cases, the belief becomes a self-fulfilling prophecy. The problem is that often we are unaware of our beliefs and how they affect our actions.

How are beliefs created? We think a dozen times before choosing the style and colour of our clothes. We are careful about what we decide to put into our stomach. However, our beliefs, which are more important than food and clothes, seem to just happen to us. Well, actually, this is not so.

Some beliefs are a result of partial experience. If a student fails to qualify for the school team in two sports—cricket and tennis—he extrapolates to assume that he has no potential in sports. Factually, he may be a talented field hockey player, but a double-negative experience made him lose faith in his abilities.

Other beliefs develop from hearsay. Five friends tell you they doubled their assets in four years by investing in real estate. You immediately jump to the conclusion, 'If four of them are saying so, they must be right.' In reality, they may have all been lucky to ride an expansion wave, but you established your belief based on what others said.

Is changing beliefs in our hands? Let us say, I offer you ₹1 crore, on the condition that within the next five minutes, you will believe you can fly at a height of 10 feet from the ground. Would you be able to develop the belief and claim your prize money? No matter how much you tried, your intellect would refuse to allow the conviction to take root.

Changing beliefs is not easy! What, then, can we do to develop empowering convictions? Here is a three-step formula.

Śhravaṇ—hear or read divine knowledge. This illumines us with the wisdom of the scriptures. Depending on your interest, this could include the study of the scriptures or listening to the words of your own Guru. You could also take advantage of the wonderful works of the many past saints in history.

Manan—**contemplate.** After hearing, the next step is to retain the wisdom. This requires internalizing it through contemplation, also known as *chintan*. It means 'to repeatedly revise a piece of knowledge with our intellect'.

For example, we know that anger is bad for us, but when enraged, we lash out. The mistake happens because the wisdom that anger is bad slips out of our intellect. If we wish to utilize our knowledge, we must keep it fresh through revision. This is accomplished by contemplation.

Nididhyāsan—**decide firmly with your intellect.** This is a conscious effort to convert knowledge into belief. For example, we may know that worldly fame is not a true source of happiness, and yet, we run after it. The reason is that the intellect does not completely believe in it. So, we must now repeatedly decide, 'This is the truth', until it becomes a conviction.

This is the three-step formula stated in the Upanishads for establishing sound beliefs—*śhravaṇ, manan* and *nididhyāsan*.

14

Partake the Wisdom of the Holy Scriptures

Humans are the only species on earth who walk with their spine erect. We have our feet on the earth and our head in the skies. This also symbolizes the conflict we face—we are endowed with a lower nature and a higher self. We possess an animalistic propensity alongside a divine nature. Our lower self seeks the physical pleasures of the senses, while our higher self aspires for divine virtues. This results in the inner battle to control sensual impulses for achieving higher goals. To this end, God has given us *vivek* (power of discernment). It is the ability to distinguish between our higher and lower urges. **An essential part of being human is to practise discernment between right and wrong at all times.**

Yoga of the intellect. One of our primary duties in life is to seek and acquire excellent wisdom. In the Bhagavad Gita, Lord Krishna tells Arjun that He is teaching him *Buddhi Yog*. It is the science of using one's intellect to rein in the urges of the mind and senses. This is where the ancient books of knowledge become vitally important.

Descending vs ascending knowledge. Millions of books get published every year. These are works of the human intellect.

Though useful in their respective subjects, they are insufficient for knowing the Absolute Truth.

They are products of mortal intellects. Hence, their knowledge is confined to the limits of the writer's understanding. They are also subject to all the flaws of human thinking, such as presumption, illusion, pride and misjudgement. These are instances of ascending knowledge—which strives to know the Truth using a bottoms-up approach.

In contrast is descending knowledge. It is that which is received as revelation from a divine and flawless source. Hence, it is perfect in the first instance. For example, consider the Bhagavad Gita. Astonishingly, while scientific theories keep changing with time, the perennial truths of the Gita remain the same. If you study the Bhagavad Gita, you will find that it is as relevant today as it was 5,000 years ago.

This amazing fact itself should lead us to believe that these holy books are coming from a Higher Source. Some were written by elevated sages after realizing the most profound truths of life through their spiritual practices. Others were direct revelations from God, received by sages in samadhi and then passed down from master to disciple.

Vedas—India's ancient and divine treasure. One of the biggest wealths of the Indian tradition is the Vedas and their related books. Together, they are called the Vedic scriptures. They are a veritable ocean of supreme wisdom. If we read them with faith, we will discover in them sublime secrets of the highest level. Even western scholars do not fail to get impressed by the Vedic scriptures.

In the great books of India, an empire spoke to us,
nothing small or unworthy, but large, serene, consistent,
the voice of an old intelligence.

—Ralph Waldo Emerson, lecturer and philosopher

Partake from the fountain of wisdom. Taking inspiration from
philosophers like Emerson, let us also establish a daily habit of
savouring the sublime knowledge of the scriptures.

While there are hundreds of sacred ancient Indian books,
I would recommend you first read these three because they
are the easiest to understand. They provide the most essential
spiritual knowledge you need. These three scriptures are:
1) Bhagavad Gita, 2) Ramayan and 3) Shreemad Bhagavatam.

If you wish to delve deeper into the secrets of the holy texts,
you will need a Guru. The Vedas themselves state: *āchāryavān
puruṣho hi veda* 'Understand Vedic knowledge under the
guidance of a Guru.' Read about the Guru in the next chapter.

15

Find a True Guru

The Guru is our guide on our journey to the highest perfection. Etymologically, the word 'Guru' contains two syllables—*gu* and *ru*. *Gu* means 'darkness' and *ru* means 'one who destroys'. Thus, the Guru is one who destroys the darkness of our ignorance and brings us to the light of divine knowledge.

The need for a Guru. In school and college, we learn with the help of textbooks and teachers. Similarly, the Vedic scriptures are like the textbooks, while the Guru is the teacher who explains them to us. He distils the essence of the scriptural knowledge, which is like divine nectar, and gifts that sublime ambrosia to us.

The Guru helps transcend obstacles. After receiving theoretical knowledge, we begin practising through sadhana. Here again, we encounter several difficulties. Once again, the Guru comes to our rescue. He encourages us; he forewarns us of the dangers; he shows us the easiest pathways; and he inspires us by his example.

Once we decide we need a Guru, we must then seek to connect with one.

Finding a true Guru. The Vedas inform us that the spiritual teacher must possess two essential qualities:

tad-vijñānārtham̐ sa gurum evābhigacchet
samit-pāṇih śrotriyam̐ brahma-niṣṭham

(*Mundakopanishad* 1.2.12)

This Vedic mantra tells us to approach a Guru who possesses two qualifications. 1) He should be well-versed in the theoretical knowledge of the scriptures, and 2) he must be situated in the realization of the Truth.

But how do we find such a personality? This is a huge challenge— first, because true saints are so few in the world, and second, because it is not easy to recognize them. We do not have a way to judge who is situated in transcendence, and who is not. I have dealt with this topic in detail in my book, *7 Divine Laws to Awaken Your Best Self.* However, I will mention a shortcut here.

Let God guide you to your Guru. The Almighty is seated in your heart and knows your deepest aspiration. When He sees that your desire to reach Him is sincere, He will lead you to a divine saint. He will also create the faith within you towards your Guru, so that you accept his guidance.

However, there is a disclaimer here. If our desire is for worldly gains, then God develops our faith in a wrong Guru. And later when we get cheated, we will blame the Guru for deceiving us, without realizing that it was our own impure desire that led to it.

Therefore, first develop a sincere yearning to love, reach and attain the Supreme Almighty. Second, pray to Him: 'O Lord! I know the purpose of life is to attain You, and for that a Guru is indispensable. But I do not have the ability to find such a saint.

Please guide me to my Spiritual Mentor.'

Surrender to the Guru. Connecting with a genuine Guru is only the beginning of the journey. Next, you must follow his instructions.

If ever we fall sick, we visit a doctor. We submit our understanding to her. Since she is a specialist in medical science, she diagnoses our ailment and prescribes the remedy accordingly.

Now, for the treatment to work, we must follow the doctor's instructions faithfully. Since the doctor is a specialist—while we have no knowledge of medicine—we willingly surrender our intellect and undergo treatment, as prescribed.

Likewise, the Guru is a spiritual doctor. We go to him as *bhav-rog* patients—souls afflicted by maya. But if we insist on doing things by the wisdom of our intellect, the relationship with our Guru becomes meaningless. He can only cure us if we submit to his advice. And only then, does the miracle of life transformation take place.

16

Imbibe Goodness Through Satsang

The company we keep has the power to influence us in remarkable ways. In fact, the scriptures compare our heart to a crystal. It reflects the qualities of the people we spend significant time with.

Motivational speaker, entrepreneur and author Jim Rohn expressed it well: 'You are the average of the five people you spend most time with.' Our company determines the activities we get regularly exposed to; it influences the conversations we engage in; and the beliefs that we uphold. Consequently, we, too, begin to think and act like our friends.

Some people lift you up in life, while others drag you downhill. If your companions are money-minded, their lust for wealth will infect you. Conversely, if they prioritize integrity and virtue, you will start holding these in high regard yourself. If your associates are health conscious, you will likely start exercising as they do. But if they love tamasic entertainment, you will end up spending time in discotheques and roadside eateries.

Associate with people you admire. If you wish to lead a positive life, then choose friends from whom you can learn and grow. They are already how you wish to become. Their mindsets, values and beliefs will naturally rub off on you.

By the same logic, if you aspire for inner transformation, then you must associate with saintly-minded people. While worldly association will keep you entangled in material consciousness, association with holy personalities will lift you to sublime heights. Sage Tulsidas said:

ek ghaḍī ādhī ghaḍī, ādhī meṅ puni ādh,
tulsī sangat sādhu kī, koṭi kaṭe aparādh

'The association of holy people is so compelling that even a few moments of it can destroy stockpiles of our past sins.' Such association is called 'satsang'.

Satsang. The word *sat* means 'Truth' and *saṅg* implies 'to associate with'. Therefore, 'satsang' means to associate with holy personalities. This can be in several ways:

- through physical association (*vapu*),
- by hearing their words and teachings (*vāṇī*), and
- by meditating on their divine personality or sublime messages (dhyan).

Devotional gatherings and activities. Associating with spiritual groups, such as those in temples and ashrams, is a wonderful means of engaging in satsang. Here, you get to be in the company of people who practise humbleness, virtue and faith. People who have positivity and devotion. People who bring sacred thoughts to their mind. Their bhakti (loving devotion) and *sevā* bhav (sentiments of service) will naturally infect you.

Satsang also provides an avenue for engaging in devotional

activities—kirtans (chanting), discourses, meditation and
sevā. Left to ourselves, we may become careless and neglect
our sadhana. But in the company of other aspirants, we find a
steady source of inspiration for our spiritual endeavours.

Satsang strengthens our faith. A prerequisite for developing
bhakti is *śhraddhā* (faith). But what should they do who do not
possess faith? Sage Ved Vyas assures them of a way:

> *satāṁ prasaṅgān mama vīrya-saṁvido,*
> *bhavanti hṛit-karṇa-rasāyanāḥ kathāḥ*
> *taj-joṣhaṇād āśhv apavarga-vartmani*
> *śhraddhā ratir bhaktir anukramiṣhyati*
>
> (Bhagavatam 3.25.25)

'Participate in the satsang of elevated souls. Hear from them
discussions on divine topics that are pleasing to the heart. Their
association will gradually evoke faith, interest and devotion
in you.'

Do make satsang a part of your life and experience its incredible
benefits. Over the last three decades, I have repeatedly witnessed
thousands of seekers completely transform their lives through
satsang. It all began with the first step they took, which was to
join a weekly spiritual congregation.

17

Set Up Your Daily Practice of Sadhana

We face so many distractions all around which demand our time and attention. What is the way to grow spiritually in the midst of these disruptions and duties?

The answer is simple. Dedicate an hour for daily sadhana. During this period, shut out all worldly disturbances to engage your mind and intellect in spiritual disciplines. It will enable you to go within yourself and access deeper mental states. The Bhagavad Gita recommends going into isolation every day:

vivikta sevī laghv-āśhī   (18.52)

'Practise these teachings in a secluded place.' Free from distracting externals, you can focus on uplifting your thoughts to God and establish His living presence in your heart.

Compare this to exercise—sedentary workers realize how necessary it is for staying fit. If they do not incorporate some form of physical exercise into their schedule, they cannot sustain good health. Similarly, your daily sadhana is spiritual exercise for the health of your mind and intellect.

Perfection is a consequence of training. The 'monkey' mind can play mischief and wander aimlessly when we try to engage in sadhana. Yet, we have to persist by repeatedly bringing it back. Maharishi Patanjali states in his *Yog Darshan*:

abhyāsa vairāgyābhyāṁ tannirodhaḥ   (sutra 1.12)

'The perturbations of the mind can be controlled by constant practise and detachment.' So, whether it be the struggle to wake up early or focus the mind on the desired object of meditation, you have to practise these repeatedly.

Do not let failure discourage you. Remember that the integration of any new behavioural pattern is initially difficult. As you stick to it, you will fall into a habit, until the point of automaticity is reached. At that stage, it will become effortless. You will feel immense bliss from within and manifest the transformation you seek. Hence, do not be discouraged by failed attempts. Keep moving forward with enthusiasm to gain proficiency in your daily spiritual routine.

The sadhana format. What should you do during the one-hour period? Here is the **KripaluPadhati** format I recommend for a 60-minute practice of sadhana. You are welcome to start with a shorter duration of each activity and slowly progress towards one hour.

5 minutes – *Prārthanā* (prayer)

10 minutes – Roop Dhyan meditation

20 minutes – *Śhravaṇ* (listen to a lecture)

20 minutes – Kirtan (chanting, hearing, remembering)

5 minutes – *Āratī* (ceremony of lights)

60 minutes – Total duration

Each of the techniques listed above is immensely transformational. I am saying that because I have taught them to millions of people around the world and seen how they benefitted from them. You, too, can utilize them to reach the supreme goal of your life.

To help you practise on the lines of the above 60-minute format, JKYog offers an online course titled *Daily Sadhana*. You can access it at *www.mydailysadhana.org*. It is a unique online spiritual platform for seekers of all backgrounds to make regular spiritual progress at their own pace and in the comfort of their home. With its help, you can practise spirituality every day in a structured and engaging manner.

18

Purifying Your Mind Is the Key

While practising spirituality, very often, we make a vital mistake. We perform poojas (sacred rituals) physically, but do not make our thoughts devotional. We sing bhajans with our tongue, but the mind worries about work at the office. We chant the Names of God, while desires for mouth-watering foods dominate our consciousness. In other words, we do bhakti externally but inwardly remain engrossed in worldly thoughts. Consequently, we miss out on the blessings galore.

Physical devotion is not sufficient. Until our mind gets purified, we will not get the divine bliss we covet. And until our mind becomes absorbed in God, it will not get purified. The Shreemad Bhagavatam informs us:

chetaḥ khalv asya bandhāya muktaye chātmano matam

guṇeṣhu saktaṁ bandhāya rataṁ vā puṁsi muktaye

(3.25.15)

'Know it without doubt that the state of the mind determines both bondage in maya, and liberation from it. When attached to the world, it results in bondage; but when absorbed in God, it causes salvation.'

Your internal intention is what matters. God is sitting within; He notes what you think. Thus, from a spiritual perspective, the internal intention is important. This is the opposite of the worldly perspective. The world does not know your thoughts; it sees your behaviour and judges you by it. That is why people put on an external show of goodness.

Let us say, Haridutt goes to Vishnudutt's home. Vishnudutt sees him, and thinks, 'O my God! This nuisance has come.'

However, he remembers that his file is on Haridutt's desk for approval, so he hides his feelings and puts on a superficial act of hospitality. 'Come...come...come, Haridutt! It's been such a long time. I was about to call you over this week anyway.'

Haridutt does not know Vishnudutt's heart. Hence, the external display of goodness impresses him, and he thinks, 'My friend, Vishnudutt, loves me so much. He has been looking forward to getting together.'

These kinds of empty acts of goodness succeed in the world, but they do not work with God. If we recite prayers to Him with our mind absorbed in material things, it is like multiplication in zeros. Whether you multiply 100 with zero or 1,000 with zero, the result is the same—zero. Similarly, whether we do bhakti for 10 minutes or for an hour, if our mind is in the world, it all amounts to zero.

Can a bath in the Ganga wash away our sins? *People ask me this question, 'Swamiji, our scriptures say that if we bathe in the holy Ganga, our sins will be washed away. But I have taken the sacred bath so many times. Why were my sins not washed away?'*

*In response to their question, I ask them to introspect where their
mind was while they were bathing their body in the sacred waters.
It was immersed in trivial matters: 'Oh...I left my wallet in the
trouser pocket. I must keep an eye on it, lest someone steals it',
'Ugh...the water is ice-cold. I am shivering', 'There is a cute child
bathing', and so on.*

They only cleaned their body, while the mind remained in
the world. The cleansing of the mind and its ugly thoughts
would have happened with divine sentiments: 'This water has
emanated from the lotus feet of Lord Narayan. I am blessed
to anoint myself in it.' Without the accompanying bhav
(sentiments), a mere bath in the Ganga was an empty drill.

When we add such divine sentiments to ritualistic ceremonies
and sacred baths, they become meaningful devotional practices.
But when the bhav is ignored, what remains is a hollow ritual.

Focus on your bhav. Always strive to adorn your mind with
devotional sentiments. It can be done in a variety of ways. Here
are a few simple examples.

- *While singing kirtans, think, 'My Sita Ram are standing before
  me and listening to my bhajan. Let me sing with all my heart
  for Their pleasure.'*
- *If worshipping deities, think, 'Radha Krishna so graciously
  reside in my home in this form. I am blessed with the
  opportunity to serve Them.'*
- *When offering prayers, create the sentiment, 'O Lord, I try
  to keep my thoughts in You, but I fail. I have no other means
  now, apart from Your grace. Please bless me and attach my
  mind to Your lotus feet.'*

- *If reading the* Bhagavad Gita, *or similar holy books, feel, 'These sacred words emanated from the mouth of the Supreme Divine Personality. I am so fortunate to read the Song of God.'*

These are just a few examples of bhav. Likewise, strive to keep decorating your emotions and cultivating higher ones. Remember, there is no limit to how devotional you can make your thoughts. The nature of bhakti is to always feel, 'My bhav towards Him is still not good enough. I must work on beautifying my emotions even further.'

Above, I have given only the tiniest sample of the wonderful devotional sentiments you can cultivate. While doing your devotion and pooja, keep your mind in God. As your bhav develops in intensity, your connection with the Lord will grow deeper and deeper, and the bliss of bhakti will become sweeter and sweeter.

19

How to Meditate

Meditation is India's gift to the world. The Sanskrit word for it is 'dhyan'. When Buddhism travelled from India to China, the word 'dhyan' got modified to *jhan,* and later to Zen, which became a popular school of Mahayana Buddhism.

Yet, in the West, meditation remained practically unknown until about 125 years ago. Since then, a spate of spiritual teachers who came over from India, brought it with them and taught it to the western world. Today, it has become widely accepted as an elite activity. Because of its immense benefits, it is practised in corporate boardrooms, universities, peak-performance training and wellness clinics, to name a few places.

The goal of meditation. True benefits of meditation extend far beyond enhancing concentration or developing focus. It is a tool for going within yourself, enabling you to work on your mind, intellect and ego, thereby uplifting your consciousness.

Some look on meditation as a way to bathe their mind in noble thoughts. Others utilize it to achieve the state of thoughtlessness, or *nirvikalpa samadhi*. Yet others practise the technique as a means for reaching God.

Various styles of meditation. Literally thousands of techniques of dhyan exist. In his *Yog Sutras*, Maharshi Patanjali mentions a few of these ways:

- Meditate on the syllable 'Om'. (sutra 1.27)
- Meditate upon the Names of God, along with divine sentiments. (sutra 1.28)
- Concentrate on a single truth. (sutra 1.32)
- Regulate the breath, particularly attending to the exhalation. (sutra 1.34)
- Contemplate upon any chosen object. (sutra 1.35)
- Stabilize the mind upon the Supreme, who is beyond sorrow. (sutra 1.36)
- Meditate upon the Guru, the illumined one free from cravings. (sutra 1.37)
- Recollect the experience of dream and deep sleep. (sutra 1.38)
- Meditate on any divine form that you revere. (sutra 1.39)

The above list is a small sample of the innumerable kinds of meditation that are possible.

What is the correct posture for meditation? Adopt any posture that you find comfortable. But ensure that you can sit comfortably in it for the period of the meditation, without undue strain to yourself.

When is the best time to meditate? Morning is considered the best time to meditate since the mind is quiet and fresh. Some prefer to do it as the last thing at night before falling asleep. If these do not work for you, allocate any other time that suits you.

Where should you meditate? It is best to keep a designated corner, preferably the place where you have set up an altar for your pooja and prayers. If you are wondering about which direction to face, remember that God is omnipresent; it is fine to face any direction while meditating.

The common problem in meditation is our distracted mind. It does not wish to sit still even for a moment. Its nature is to generate thoughts, and it likes to do so even when we sit for dhyan. Consequently, the mind runs helter-skelter, and these fluctuations become very discouraging for those striving to focus it.

The most effective meditational technique. To handle the restless mind, the best solution is the technique of Roop Dhyan meditation that Jagadguru Kripaluji Maharaj propagated.

Roop Dhyan—meditating upon the image of God—has two advantages. First, the form of the Lord provides an all-attractive basis for the mind to focus upon. Second, since the Lord is all-pure, the mind gets purified as well. This second benefit is extremely important because only when the mind is cleansed can it be brought under control.

Roop Dhyan comes naturally to the mind. Whenever we remember people, events and things, we bring their image to our mind. This is our nature. For example, when we think of our parents, we first remember their image, not their name. Now, in meditation, if we merely focus upon the syllable 'Om', the mind will find it difficult to stabilize. But if we have the all-attractive image of the Lord before us, the mind will effortlessly be drawn towards it. Jagadguru Shree Kripaluji Maharaj states:

sab sādhan janu deh sam, rūp dhyān janu prān

(Bhakti Śhatak verse 10)

'All spiritual practices are like the body; meditation upon the form of God is like the life-airs. (Without life-airs, the body cannot survive.)'

Here is a simple way to practise Roop Dhyan meditation.

1) Choose any form of the Lord that is appealing to you and bring His image in front of you. You can also meditate upon a deity or picture of God or create any form of His in your mind.

2) Once the mind is focused upon the divine form, you can make this practice more yielding by remembering the divine virtues of God. Think of His infinite beauty, compassion, knowledge, love or any other qualities.

3) Enliven your Roop Dhyan by imagining Him moving, talking, walking or engaging in some activity. This makes your practise enchanting and interesting.

4) You can then make your meditation even sweeter by meditating on His divine Pastimes (*leelas*). You can recall any of His infinite *leelas* or imagine your own personal Pastimes with Him.

5) Or you can serve Him in your mind! Visualize yourself worshipping Him, singing to Him, offering foodstuffs to Him, massaging His feet, cooking for Him, fanning Him, bathing Him, etc. This is called *mānasī sevā* (serving God in the mind).

Following these simple guidelines will help you easily

incorporate mediation into your daily routine. Remember, technique and procedures are only important if they assist in absorbing your mind in God. Hopefully, these instructions will help in your journey of meditation.

20

Cultivate Awareness of the Presence of God

Most of us engage in some form of daily devotion. We have our own way of doing bhakti—meditating, chanting *japa*, singing bhajans, worshipping deities, and so on. Through such devotion, we try to take our mind to God and purify it.

However, afterwards we allow our mind to fill up with worldly thoughts for the rest of the day. This neutralizes the purification we had achieved through sadhana. The level of our consciousness goes up-down, up-down, up-down. Consequently, even after decades of bhakti, we find we have not made satisfactory progress. This could be avoided if the mind always remained in God.

Karm Yog—the message of the Gita. Lord Krishna taught Arjun the concept of karm yog. In simple words it means: 'body in the world, mind in the Lord'.

Shree Krishna encouraged Arjun to be such a karm yogi. He instructed:

sarveshu kāleshu mām anusmara yudhya cha

(Bhagavad Gita 8.7)

'Remember Me at all times; keep doing your work alongside.'

The critical point here is to think of God constantly, and not forget Him for even a moment. On hearing this, people ask, 'Is that even possible? If we constantly keep thinking of Bhagavan, how can we do our worldly works?'

From Indian history we learn of many great karm yogis who lived in ancient times. Yudhishthir, Prahalad, Ambarish and Dhruv were all exemplary rulers. They performed their kingly duties with utmost sincerity. Yet, their consciousness was always absorbed in the Divine. The technique they used is the one we are going to discuss.

See the whole world as the temple of God. Most of us perceive and connect with the Divine when we visit a temple, gurudwara, church, mosque, synagogue or some other place of worship. But as soon as we walk out, we forget Him. We must now progress further and learn to see the entire world as His temple.

The Vedas tells us that God is all-pervading:

eko devaḥ sarvabhūteṣu gūḍhaḥ
sarvavyāpī sarvabhūtāntarātmā

(*Shwetashwatar Upanishad* 6.11)

'There is one Supreme Divine Personality. He resides within all living beings, for He pervades everything and is the Supreme Soul of all beings.'

We have often heard these adjectives for God. Let us now imbibe them in our consciousness by a simple technique.

God is always watching us. The big advantage of realizing

God's presence with you is that it will discourage you from unethical behaviour.

Let us say, Ramesh intends to commit a theft. He is walking on a nearby street at midnight, confident that nobody is watching him. His plan is to steal someone's scooter in the neighbourhood.

At that moment, his neighbour, Dinesh, comes from behind and pats him on the back, 'Ramesh, what are you doing here?'

Ramesh sees Dinesh is around, and so he immediately conceals his intention to sin. He blurts out, 'Oh! I was not feeling sleepy, so I was just taking a walk.'

Observe, when Ramesh realized that he was not alone, he desisted from sin. His behaviour was reformed merely from the fear that Dinesh was there.

When fear of a mere mortal watching us can make such a difference, then think of the transformation that will happen from realizing that God is always our witness. It will help us live by the highest standards of morality and ethics.

How to practise the presence of God. When we engage in any activity, we always remain aware of our 'self'. The feeling continues: 'I am walking, I am eating, I am talking', and so on. But we forget that God is also seated in our heart, and He is always watching us.

Now, think: 'I am not alone. God is always with me. He is my Witness and my Protector.'

Suppose you go to office and sit down for work. Before you get engrossed in your work, stop for a moment. There is an empty chair in front of you. Think, 'Lord Ram is sitting on that chair. He is watching me.' Realize His presence and then begin your work.

It is natural that as you get engrossed in work, God will slip out of your mind. This is because you are not yet an accomplished karm yogi. But do not be disheartened. After an hour, stop work for a moment and think, 'God is watching me.'

In this way, your consciousness, which had started slipping from the Divine to the mundane, will again get elevated. Keep the practice going, decreasing the interval to every 30 minutes, then 15 minutes, and so on. With constant practise, the stage will come when you continuously feel the presence of God with you.

This practise requires no external display. The simplicity of this technique is that it does not require the help of external props like a *japa mala* (rosary beads). Thinking and visualizing the presence of God can be done quietly and discreetly. Consequently, it does not invoke cynicism of others. It can be added to your daily life without requiring explanations and clarifications.

The beauty of practising the presence of God is that it slowly yokes the mind to Him. And the consciousness grows divine. This technique is immensely powerful and beneficial for your spiritual elevation.

21

Live Your Life with God

We all wish we had a true friend who was always there for us. The perfect companion would be someone who understood us and to whom we could open our heart without hesitation. An ideal friendship that would not fade with time, instead, grow ever fonder.

Is finding such a great friend impossible in this selfish world? Actually not! The Vedas inform us that our true Friend, God, is not even a hair's breadth away. He is sitting within our heart and is waiting for us with open arms. The delay is from our side; we have not yet learnt to make Him a part of our life. That is what we must now strive to do.

The Bhagavad Gita states God's divine law according to which He graces us:

ye yathā māṁ prapadyante tāns tathaiva bhajāmyaham

(4.11)

'As you surrender to Me, I shall reciprocate with you accordingly.' So, if we wish to receive more of His grace, we must consciously practise making Him a part of our life journey.

Benefits of living with God. Making God the centre of your life will bestow huge blessings. First, you will develop a sense of security and freedom from fear. 'When the Master of infinite universes is my Best Friend, and He is always with me, then why should I fear?'

Along with security will come hope and optimism. 'I am sure my Lord has a plan for me. I cannot see it now, but I trust Him.' Even when the going gets tough, faith in God gives us staying power. It helps us see light at the end of the tunnel.

Whenever we do anything significant, our ego suggests, 'I am special. I have achieved such wonders.' This self-conceit will also be gradually eliminated. With practise, it will get replaced by devotional sentiments as in the following Sanskrit verse:

yatkṛitaṁ yatkarishyāmi tatsarvaṁ na mayā kṛitam
tvayā kṛitaṁ tu phalabhuk tvameva madhusūdana

'Whatever I accomplished and whatever I achieve in future, O Shree Krishna, I never did any of it. You bestowed upon me the power to do it, and the fruits are for Your pleasure.'

Now that we understand the tremendous benefits of bringing God into our life, let us discuss some ways to make it happen.

Speak to God. When was the last time you spoke to God? We speak to golf balls, 'Come on! Come on! Only three more inches please.' Yet, we forget our Best Friend, who sits inside us and does not leave us for even a fraction of a second. Now, communicate with Him many times a day. Speak to God about your weaknesses. Tell Him about your dreams. Express thanks to Him for His innumerable gifts. Of course, He is aware of your

innermost desires, but talking to Him helps us become aware
of His presence.

Listen to your Friend as well. Presently, we cannot hear His
words directly, but they are available indirectly. The Supreme
Lord spoke that wisdom with His own mouth to Arjun and
through him, to all of us. Hence, the Bhagavad Gita is veritably
the Song of God (*www.holy-bhagavad-gita.org*). Read the words
of your Dearest Friend, savour their sacredness and bathe your
intellect in their wisdom.

Please Him through your works. Before any activity, recollect
yourself and think, 'I am doing this for the pleasure of my
Supreme Beloved.' This one persistent thought will purify
your intention and completely transform your consciousness.
From being self-centred, you will become God-centred.
This could be as simple as offering your food to God before
partaking it as His remnants. Or while at work, keeping the
awareness that you are performing each activity for God's
happiness.

Whenever you complete an activity to take up another, make
it a habit to pause for a moment. Thank God for His grace that
enabled you to do it. Think of any learning or wisdom gained
in the process. Then offer the results and outcomes to Him,
for His pleasure.

Place your doubts before Him. Whenever a big or small
dilemma arises, turn to Him and request a resolution. Before
you seek answers from the world, place the questions that
puzzle you before your Best Friend. He is the God of love, and
He appreciates that you see Him and His representative, the

Guru, as your exclusive shelter. He reciprocates your faith and trust, by gracing you in inconceivable ways.

The purpose of this chapter was to encourage you to commune more with your Eternal Friend and show you the potential for sweetness in your relationship with Him.

22
What Should We Ask from God?

T̶ake a little child to a jewellery shop and put a chocolate in front of her. Then tell her, 'Dear Daughter, take whatever you want.' What do you think the child will pick up? Obviously, her hand will go for the chocolates since her experience of happiness is limited to the pleasure she derives from chocolates. She has no idea of the value of the precious stones and yellow metal.

Similarly, in the realm of spirituality, we are like little children. Since endless lifetimes, we have only experienced worldly happiness. We have no idea of different kinds of divine bliss—such as *Brahmānand* (bliss of the formless aspect of God) and *Premānand* (bliss of the personal form of God)—which are infinitely sweeter than material pleasures. If we are asked to choose what we want from God, we will likely ask for worthless trinkets. Chaitanya Mahaprabhu explained:

kṛishṇa kahe, — 'āmā bhaje, mānge viṣhaya-sukh
amṛit chhāḍi' viṣha mānge — ei baḍa mūrkh

(*Chaitanya Charitamrit, Madhya Leela*, 22.38)

Lord Krishna says, 'This soul has come to Me and is asking for sensual pleasures. It is like reaching the ocean of nectar but asking for poison.'

If you wish to avoid this foolish mistake, you can adopt a simple solution. Pray in this manner:

merī chāhī mat karo main mūrakh ajñān,
terī chāhī men prabhu hai merā kalyān

'O Lord, I am ignorant and do not know what is good for me. You please decide what is in my best interest.' When we leave it in the hands of the Divine, He becomes obliged to ascertain our welfare and grant us the most beneficial thing. This is the smart way to pray.

Do not do business with the Lord. The concept of 'give and take' comes very naturally to us. We do it in the world, and when we engage in devotion, we do the same. 'O Ma Vaishno Devi, if You get my daughter married, I will donate a gold ring at the temple.' 'O Lord Venkatesh, I will feed one hundred brahmins, if You improve my health.'

However, this is not true bhakti. It is tantamount to trading with God because the intention remains, 'What will I get in return?' This is why, it is not love; it is business.

The three kinds of affection—love, lust and business.

1) Where the goal is 'take...take...take', that is lust.

2) Where the goal is 'give and take...give and take', that is business.

3) Where the goal is 'give...give...give', that is divine love.

I do not need to mention that the highest amongst the three is divine love. When it is directed towards God, it is called *nishkām bhakti* (selfless devotion).

If you wish to practise *niṣhkām bhakti*, then do not think what you can get from the Lord. Instead, think of how you can serve Him with *tan, man* and *dhan* (body, mind and wealth). The beauty is that when you make giving as your goal, God will give everything to you. As the saying goes: *bin māṅge motī mile, māṅge mile na bhīkh* 'On asking, you get nothing. If you stop asking, you get priceless gems.'

It is straightforward logic. God loves us and is eager to grace us. However, He waits for us to become selfless before He decides to shower His infinite bliss, knowledge and love.

The highest prayer. Keeping in mind the above divine principle, you should strive to increase your service attitude. Then, align your prayer accordingly.

Pray for bhakti, so that you may be able to serve Him with selfless love. Pray for wisdom, so that you may learn to follow His will. Pray for detachment, so that you may free your mind and engage it in His thoughts. Pray for inspiration, so that you may please Him by moving ahead quickly on the path. Pray for strength, so that you can engage in His tireless service.

When the intention behind your prayer is loving devotion and service to God, it becomes a selfless prayer because it is not self-seeking. This is the highest form of prayer.

Section Two

GOOD HEALTH AND WELL-BEING

23

Prioritize Your Health

To lead a happy and effective life—a quality life—you must take care of its key critical areas. As discussed in the introduction to the book, for most people, these are profession, health, relationships, finances and spirituality. Disruption in any of these makes life problematic and frustrating.

Amongst these five, health often becomes the limiting one. Even minor health issues—like aches, allergy and lethargy—can bring you to a standstill. We all have had the experience of spending a day in bed because of an ailment, while our work lay sabotaged. Hence, the ancient poet Mahakavi Kalidas stated:

śharīra mādhyam khalu dharma sādhanam
(*Kumarasambhavam Sarga* 5.33)

'Your body is the means for doing good works.'

Despite its paramount importance, this vital aspect of life gets neglected amidst the hustle and bustle of everyday existence. Whether you are a corporate executive, an entrepreneur or a busy homemaker, healthy habits tend to take a back seat before the excessive demands of work.

However, the consequences of such negligence are drastic. Towards the end of middle age, a variety of diseases start rearing their head—hypertension, diabetes, backaches and even cardiac issues. Then, when old age sets in and the body is besieged with afflictions, the realization dawns that disregarding health was a big mistake. But by then it is too late.

The Institute for Aerobics Research conducted an eight-year study of 13,000 people to review the correlation between walking and death rate. It revealed that those who walked just 30 minutes a day reduced their chances of dying prematurely when compared with those who exercised infrequently. The key takeaway was that merely by incorporating the habit of spending a half hour on exercise every day, you can significantly improve your health.[7]

Hence, do not delay in instilling healthy habits that bestow well-being and longevity. They may be hard to develop because they require making small sacrifices. But if you are willing to tolerate the inconvenience, the benefits you reap will be immense. Likewise, unhealthy habits will be tough to break, but once you overcome them, your life will be filled with new vigour.

In following healthy habits, Jagadguru Kripaluji Maharaj was an ideal role model. As a descended saint, he could easily have taken care of his body, merely with the help of divine powers, even without adhering to healthful ways. Yet, until the ripe age of 92, he diligently followed all the principles of holistic well-being, while working 24/7 for the welfare of humankind.

In this section, we will discuss the most important healthy and harmful practices. These will deepen your knowledge about the proper way for exercise, nutrition, relaxation, mental health and hygiene.

---

[7]American Council on Exercise, 'A Walk a Day', 8 January 2009, https://bit.ly/3PA2XUV. Accessed on 25 June 2022.

24

A Balanced Diet Is the Best Diet

Every other day, a new diet becomes the fad, with its tall claims as a one-stop solution to all our physical woes. These fad diets offer flashy promises of quick weight loss and good health, luring gullible people to fall prey. They often tout extreme plans that eliminate major food groups, leading to deficiencies in our body. As a result, the body is deprived of essential nutrients, which becomes the precursor of disease. Some diets lead to kidney stones, heart disease or constipation. Many end with fatigue, frustration and eventually failure. Most are unrealistic to live with, and some are outright dangerous for our health.

However, healthy eating is not difficult to practise if we follow conventional wisdom and adopt a balanced approach to nutrition. Yes, it is just so simple! Eating a balanced and varied diet is the best approach to good health. It is one that provides all the nutrients for our body's requirements, in the right proportions. It is undoubtedly the most sensible diet plan you can follow.

Let us look at each of the components of a healthy balanced diet. Do keep in mind that this topic is vast, but within the scope of this book, I have kept the discussion brief. Refer to my book,

Science of Healthy Diet for a complete overview of good eating habits, food groups and nutrition.

I HAVE A BALANCED DIET.
I HAVE THREE-COURSE MEALS
THREE TIMES A DAY

We will start with the macronutrients. These are nutrients our body needs in large quantities—proteins, carbohydrates (carbs) and fats.

Proteins. They are the main building blocks of our body like bricks that go into building a house. Proteins are required for growth and regeneration of cells and tissues. They form a large component of muscle tissues in the body. They are also the essential component of the immune system. Further, our body also uses them as an alternative energy source.

Proteins are made of molecules called amino acids that link together to form chains. Amino acids can be of two kinds:

essential and non-essential. Our body produces the latter, while the former are obtained through the diet.

The RDA (Recommended Dietary Allowance) is 0.8 grams of protein per kilogram of body weight per day. In general, women require an average of 46 grams and men around 56 grams daily. Note that one gram of protein equals four calories. For adults over the age of 19, the United States Department of Agriculture (USDA) recommends that 10–35 per cent of your caloric intake should be from proteins.

Legumes, including lentils, beans and pulses, are a rich source of proteins. Nuts such as almonds, peanuts and cashews are also excellent sources. Other vegetarian sources loaded with proteins include soyabean and dairy products.

Carbohydrates. They are the primary source of energy for the body, much like the fuel that powers an engine. Though often maligned in trendy diets, they are essential to a balanced diet. They provide operational energy to our muscles, organs and the central nervous system. They also prevent proteins from being used as an energy source and enable fat metabolism.

Carbohydrate requirements vary depending on your gender, age and activity level. However, as a general guideline, 40–60 per cent of your daily calories should be from carbohydrates. Since one gram of carbohydrate equals four calories, it translates to approximately 200–300 grams of carbs if consuming 2,000 calories per day. People with diabetes must restrict their carb intake to within 200 grams.

Carbohydrates are of various kinds—some simple and others

complex. The difference between the two is in their chemical structure and how quickly they get digested to release energy. Sugars are simple carbohydrates that are easily broken down and give instant glucose. Fibre and starches are complex carbohydrates that take time to digest and provide long-lasting energy.

Processed carbs found in candies, table sugar, namkeens, cakes and pastries are stripped of fibre. They have a higher glycaemic load, which means, they result in a sudden spike in blood sugar. Healthy carbohydrates are those that are unprocessed, low in sugar and fat, and high in fibre.

Complex carbs are found in starches including grains, pasta, bread, rice and vegetables like peas, corn, potatoes, squash and lentils. Fibre-rich complex carbs such as in fruits, nuts, beans, lentils and whole grains are also excellent sources. These are important for bowel regularity and controlling cholesterol.

Fats. They give shape to the body. They provide insulation and protection to the organs. They help store and transport fat-soluble vitamins. They are also an alternative source of energy for the body.

The USDA and the American Heart Association (AHA) recommend that for adults, 25–35 per cent of daily calories should come from fat. Since one gram of fat produces nine calories, the daily intake of fats should be in the range of 44–77 grams. However, the caveat is to consume healthy fats.

A popular myth looks on all fats as being bad for health.

However, not all fats are equal. There are three types: saturated, unsaturated and trans fats.

- **Saturated fats** are generally solid at room temperature. They are present in dairy products—milk, butter, ghee, paneer (cheese), and the like. While saturated fats support brain and neurological function, consume them sparingly as they increase bad cholesterol when taken in excess.

- **Unsaturated fats** are usually liquid at room temperature. These are further classified into monounsaturated and polyunsaturated. When taken in moderation, both are considered good and healthy. They are beneficial as they decrease bad cholesterol (LDL, low-density lipoprotein) and increase good cholesterol (HDL, high-density lipoprotein).

  Good sources of monounsaturated fats include most nuts (especially almonds), seeds, avocados and olive oil. Polyunsaturated fats are found in flaxseed, walnuts and most vegetable oils.

- **Trans fats** are artificial—they are the byproduct of hydrogenation, which turns vegetable oils into solids. You can spot them as 'partially hydrogenated oils' on the ingredients list. These are extremely damaging as they increase bad cholesterol and triglycerides in the system, and cause inflammation. They are to be shunned. Trans fats are often found in pre-made foods, cookies, fries, doughnuts, frozen pizza, etc.

We will now look at micronutrients. These are required in small amounts but are essential for body functions. They include vitamins and minerals.

Vitamins. They are necessary for growth, maintenance and regular body functions. They contribute greatly to immunity and prevention of diseases. There are 13 essential vitamins for the body and can be either water-soluble or fat-soluble.

- Water-soluble vitamins B and C are directly absorbed into the bloodstream upon digestion and need regular replenishment. They are mainly responsible for energy, metabolism and prevention of cell damage, and are required to create red blood cells. Good sources of vitamin B include fresh fruits, vegetables, whole grains, nuts and cheese. Rich sources of vitamin C include fresh fruits, such as *āmlā* (Indian gooseberry), berries, oranges and leafy green vegetables, including kale, spinach and mustard.

- Fat-soluble vitamins A, D, E and K do not dissolve in water and are best absorbed when consumed with a source of fat. They are stored in the body for future use. Together, they keep our eyes, skin, lungs, GI (gastrointestinal) tract and nervous system in good condition. In general, you can obtain these from a mixture of vegetables, seeds, nuts and whole grains. Vitamin D is mainly obtained through the skin, diet or supplements.

Minerals are of two kinds: macrominerals and micro (trace) minerals. Macrominerals include calcium, phosphorus, magnesium, sodium, potassium, sulphur and chlorine. They have varied functions including electrolyte balance, bone health, nerve transmission and regulation of blood pressure.

Milk products, leafy greens, lentils, bananas, etc. are all good sources of many minerals. Trace minerals include iron, zinc, copper, manganese, selenium, etc. Though required in trace amounts, they serve many important functions: supplying oxygen to cells, connective tissue formation and defence against oxidative damage. As with many micronutrients, they are readily available in fruits, vegetables, nuts, lentils, dairy, and the like.

Antioxidants. The process of digestion produces, as a byproduct, a small percentage of free radicals. These are also produced as reaction to environmental factors, such as smoke and radiation. Since these free radicals are unstable, they seek to neutralize themselves by corroding cells and tissues. Consequently, they lead to damage and disease. Cancer, heart disease, inflammatory conditions and many other conditions are linked to them.

Antioxidants neutralize oxidative damage to the body. Many of the fruits, particularly the dark-coloured ones are rich in antioxidants. For example, blue and purple fruits contain anthocyanin. One notable superfood with high amounts of antioxidants is the *āmlā*.

The above discussion will help you appreciate how micronutrients come to your rescue and bestow good health. Both macro- and micro-nutrients are the backbone of good health. Their intake requires a balanced diet. For a healthy lifestyle, eat approximately five servings of fruits and vegetables a day. Include vegetable protein in the form of legumes, beans, nuts and dairy. Restrict yourself to healthy low-sugar complex carbs, unprocessed foods and fibrous grains. Snack on nutritious fats from nuts and seeds, and use unsaturated oils for cooking.

25

Stay Hydrated to Stay Happy

Have you ever wondered how long can a human survive without water? It is said that we can go without food for as long as 21 days, but water is a different story. So much so that W.H. Auden, a British-American poet, said, 'Thousands have lived without love but none without water.' Water is such a vital requirement for life that an ordinary person cannot survive for more than three days without it. Lack of water causes dehydration, where the body does not have sufficient fluids to carry on its normal functions. This results in extreme thirst, fatigue, organ failure and ultimately death.

Why the body needs water. It is a well-known fact that the human body is composed of roughly 60 per cent water. Our blood is about 90 per cent water. It is an important nutrient for all bodily activities, like regulating body temperature, aiding digestion, balancing body pH, lubricating joints, eliminating toxins and delivering oxygen throughout the body.

We do not realize but during the day, our bodies keep losing water through excretion, sweating and breathing. Therefore, replenishing water in our body becomes important. The general recommendation is to drink eight glasses of water every day. However, your daily water intake can depend on several factors like level of activity, climate, age and gender.

Staying hydrated is good for health. Drinking sufficient water aids digestion and prevents constipation. When the water intake is insufficient, your body absorbs water from your colon leaving your stools hard, dry and difficult to pass. Staying hydrated keeps the bowels moving.

Dehydration can make you feel tired, since it impacts the flow of oxygen to the brain. That causes the heart to work harder in pumping blood to the bodily organs, leading to tiredness and listlessness. If you are feeling drained and fatigued, drinking water can boost your energy levels. It can also help reduce headaches caused by dehydration.

Moreover, dehydration leads to higher cortisol levels—the stress hormone. Conversely, staying hydrated helps improve one's mood. Water is also a natural appetite suppressant. Besides, it speeds up metabolism and aids in overall weight loss.

Drinking water also increases the fluid that passes through the kidneys as urine. This helps prevent mineral concentration that could later develop into kidney stones.

Keep an eye on the colour of your urine. It is the best indicator of your water intake. It should remain colourless or light yellow. A deeper colour could be a warning bell that you are getting dehydrated.

Ensure sufficient water intake. It is hard to keep track of your water intake when you are busy throughout the day. So, here are a few simple tips and tricks that will help take care of your water requirement:

- Always choose water over soda and other aerated drinks.
- Drink a glass of water after every bathroom break.
- Carry a water bottle with you wherever you go.
- Drinking water infused with lemon, mint, berries or fruit enhances their flavour and at the same time regulates the pH levels in the body.

The ideal times of the day. It is best to drink water frequently throughout the day. You can be more mindful of your water intake after waking up in the morning. Sleep is a long period to go without any water and drinking a glass is a good way to quickly rehydrate your body. Ayurveda recommends drinking four glasses of water upon waking up as a great way to clean your digestive tract. However, that is impractical for most people, while one glass of water is easily doable.

Ayurveda also strongly dissuades from drinking water immediately after a meal, as it dilutes the gastric juices secreted for digestion. After your meal, wait for two hours before drinking a glass or two. If you cannot hold on so long, then wait for an hour. And if your thirst is uncontrollable, then take half-a-glass, halfway through the meal. It will mix with the food and not impede digestion significantly.

Likewise, half hour before your meal, drinking a glassful is a good idea. However, if you aim to lose weight, drinking a glass just before your meal helps. It reduces the appetite by filling the stomach.

Another good practice is to drink water before and after a workout. Exercise makes you sweat, and you lose water and electrolytes through sweat. The water intake keeps the body hydrated and replenishes any lost fluids.

'Water is the driving force of all nature,' said Leonardo Da Vinci. Well, it surely is the driving force of a happy and healthy life. Stay hydrated, stay happy!

26

Traditional Indian Spices and Herbs Engender Good Health

Herbs and spices are the heart and soul of Indian cuisine. They lend their unique flavours, colours and textures to enhance the taste and appearance of cooked dishes. But more than that, they are hidden treasure chests of nutrients with healing benefits and compounds packed with disease-fighting qualities, which make them invaluable for holistic well-being.

Definitions. The terms 'spices' and 'herbs' are sometimes used interchangeably. To be precise, herbs come from the non-woody leafy parts of plants, while spices are derived from all the rest—seeds, root, bark, fruit, bud, flowers and resin.

Ginger and turmeric are roots; cinnamon, a bark; garlic, a bulb; cloves are flowers; cumin, fennel and mustard are seeds; and cardamom and black pepper are fruits.

While herbs may be used fresh or dried, spices are dried and used in whole or ground forms. Some are both, spice and herb, together. For example, coriander leaves are a herb and coriander seeds are a spice.

Ayurveda. Knowledge of spices and herbs as the elixirs of health was known in the Indian culture since ancient times. The health and medicinal benefits of natural plants is beautifully documented in Ayurveda and incorporated into everyday cuisine and cooking practices. What a beautifully engineered system that takes care of our holistic health, without us even realizing it!

According to Ayurveda, spices have medicinal benefits, and as a result, were known as *auṣhadhi* or medicine. Not surprising then that Hippocrates said: 'Let food be thy medicine, and medicine be thy food.' This is why it is typically recommended that they be used sparingly. Excessive use of spices makes the food tamasic.

In Indian culture, one does not need to take a prescription turmeric pill to reduce inflammation. The use of turmeric, a treasure for good health, is inbuilt in our cuisine. Hence, the incidence of diseases like Alzheimer's remains low. On the other hand, medical science is only now beginning to understand its worth. The significance of the term 'holistic', which is so evident in our scriptures, is just starting to appear on the western horizon.

Health-promoting and medicinal properties. Spices and herbs are rich sources of phytochemicals. The high content of phenolic compounds and flavonoids fight off disease. Very often, one spice may have multiple properties and benefits. For example, turmeric is anti-inflammatory, antioxidant, antibacterial, anti-cancerous, antifungal and much more. It helps treat arthritis, diabetes and Alzheimer's. Spices and herbs have multiple benefits, but some properties may be more predominant than others. For a better overall understanding, let us first look at these attributes individually.

Antioxidants. In the chapter on balanced diet, we discussed how antioxidants remove free radicals from our body. Thereby, they strengthen immunity, delay ageing and combat cell damage due to accumulation of oxidants from the environment, food, pollution and stress. Did you know that some spices and herbs are loaded with antioxidants and are manifold times more potent than dark fruits?

The Oxygen Radical Absorbance Capacity (ORAC) Score is one measure of their strength. Cloves have an ORAC score of 314,446 in comparison to 14,000 for blueberries. Cinnamon at 267,537 and turmeric at 102,700, are also high. Ginger, cumin, mustard, mint and basil are also antioxidant rich. These superfoods are powerhouses for preventing diseases.

Additionally, this antioxidant component helps in natural food preservation. So, go ahead and generously flavour your foods with these spices. But a word of caution here. These are to be consumed only in tiny quantities. Too much can result in causing serious damage to your liver and kidneys. Also, their blood thinning properties can interfere with prescribed medicines. Consuming these as a part of cooked food is the safest strategy and one that is traditionally used in every Indian household since thousands of years.

Antibacterial, antifungal and antimicrobial. These properties are abundantly present in cloves, cinnamon and cumin. They help prevent food spoilage, food-borne diseases and infectious diseases. Hence, they are natural food preservatives and have been the subject of many scientific studies. Other spices that have been studied for these characteristics include oregano, nutmeg, basil, pepper, thyme, rosemary and ginger. Likewise, turmeric, black peppercorns, coriander, fennel and cardamom, all have antimicrobial qualities, protecting against harmful bacteria, pathogens and fungus.

Anti-inflammatory, analgesic, antiseptic and antibiotic. Inflammation is the root cause of many chronic illnesses. Spices such as turmeric, cloves and ginger, and others like cayenne and cinnamon are known to reduce inflammation, provide pain relief and improve body functioning.

Curcumin is the active ingredient in turmeric—the source of its golden yellow colour and its potent power. From everyday infections like colds to chronic pain and stiffness associated with arthritis, it works by reducing inflammation in the body. It is important to note that a pinch of black pepper increases its absorption. Overdoing it can again lead to overheating of the body. A regular intake through cooked food and supplemented by drinking 'the golden drink'—hot milk laced with turmeric— can provide the necessary dose.

Cloves, due to their compound eugenol, are used as an antiseptic for periodontal disease. They control oral bacteria. Ginger, with its main compound gingerol, is used to soothe sore muscles and throats and inflammation related to arthritis. Fresh ginger has more gingerol and is best consumed as part of the diet.

Research has shown that garlic, cloves and ginger are also natural antibiotics. Garlic may be effective against *Salmonella* and *E. coli.* Chopped or crushed garlic is better. The pungent smell of garlic due to the sulphur compound allicin imparts its medicinal properties.

Along with these, spices also have some other properties that make them beneficial for health purposes. Notable among these are:

- Sugar-regulating, as seen in cinnamon, which lowers blood sugar in diabetics.
- Immunity-boosting, as seen in tulsi (holy basil) leaves, black pepper and garlic.
- Aiding gut health and digestion, as seen in ginger and cumin.

How to use them. Yes, spices are good for health. Does that mean that upping the intake of spices whether in food or pills will help boost bodily health? That is not how it works. Spices have their heating and cooling properties. The kind, type and quantity of spices and herbs are recommended based on individual needs and the body's predispositions.

Seasons can be another determining factor. Cooling tulsi or *sabzā* seeds are recommended in summer, as opposed to warming ginger powder in the winters.

For home treatments: For simple afflictions, like coughs, colds, indigestion and stomach aches, take a soothing hot drink, or *kāḍhā*, made with boiling spices, such as cloves, ginger and black pepper, with tulsi leaves in water. Sweetened with honey or jaggery, it is an effective home remedy, blessed with nutrients to alleviate the symptoms.

Another effective therapy is to wrap a mix of dry spices in a cloth bundle, which is then heated on a griddle and applied to relieve soreness of muscles, inflammation or chest congestion.

A third prescription is to infuse any carrier oil with spices by heating, and then massaging the oil over the affected area, such as knees for arthritis pain. These are some simple home therapeutic methods.

Go ahead and put your spice rack to its best use! Equipped with an understanding of their deep-reaching benefits, you can develop your personal disease prevention system. And above all, enjoy good, healthy and tasteful aromatic-spicy foods!

27

Good Gut Health

Today, the number of people affected by gut issues is huge, with millions around the world fighting digestive disorders. The ailments could be minor, such as indigestion and constipation, or serious, like celiac disease, ulcerative colitis and Crohn's disease. These are prompting people to look at gut health more closely.

First, understand what we mean by the 'gut'. This term refers to the digestive tract; other names for it are gastrointestinal tract (GI tract) and alimentary canal. This tract is about a 30-feet long muscular tube that runs from your mouth to the anus. It includes the mouth, oesophagus, stomach, pancreas, liver, gallbladder, small intestine, colon and rectum.

Your gut is host to about 100 trillion microorganisms known as the gut microbiome, or gut flora. They perform functions such as digesting food, absorbing nutrients, regulating metabolism and immune function, and removing toxins from the body. Everyone has a unique gut flora. A diverse and mixed combination of bacteria is considered healthy.

A certain level of bad bacteria is normal in the gut. But the situation can quickly turn precarious if the balance is tipped in favour of the bad bacteria (including viruses or fungi), causing inflammation, infections and other health risks. The gut environment should be conducive to the growth and development of good bacteria and restrictive of bad.

Another interesting fact about the gut is that the GI tract and the brain are intricately connected and affect one another profoundly. The gut is governed by its system of neurons known as the Enteric Nervous System (ENS). The ENS is also known as the 'second brain', with a network of 100 million nerve cells that is in constant communication with the big brain in the skull.

You may have had instances where you felt 'butterflies in your stomach' before giving a presentation or felt nauseous at the thought of something grotesque. That is because the digestive tract is overly sensitive to emotions, especially anger, anxiety, sadness, extreme happiness, and the like. These can all trigger symptoms in the gut. The cause and effect work in both directions. Also, note that the gut produces over 90 per cent of the body's serotonin—the hormone that regulates our emotions. That is why both physiological and psychological factors play a role in GI disorders.

Further, our gut is one of the main defence systems of the body. First, the stomach acid and enzymes in the gut help sterilize the food and protect the body from infection. Second, 70 per cent of the cells that make up our immune system are in the gut. The epithelial cells of the small intestine are coated with glycoproteins that form a barrier against penetrating microbes by trapping bacteria in the mucus.

The term 'leaky gut' is used when the gut lining is damaged and cannot optimally function as a barrier any longer. The smaller holes expand and allow harmful substances like gluten, bad bacteria and undigested food particles to enter your bloodstream. This results in considerable damage to health.

Maintaining the health of your digestive tract cannot be emphasized enough. It is the epicentre of your metabolic activity affecting your physiology, metabolism, digestion, inflammation, hormonal function and immunity. For optimal health, your gut must function seamlessly.

The symptoms of an unhealthy or imbalanced gut. An imbalance or disruption in the gut microbiome is known as dysbiosis. Some of the most common symptoms in people with compromised gut bacteria include digestive problems such as constipation, diarrhoea, bloating, nausea, heartburn and vomiting. Further, unintentional weight changes, sleep disturbances, fatigue, food intolerance, skin problems and hormonal fluctuations could suggest a microbial imbalance in the gut. Latest research indicates that anxiety, depression and related disorders could potentially be related to the gut as well.[8]

How can we keep our gut flora healthy and robust? First, it is important to address some of the common factors that throw your system off balance.

---

[8]Clapp, Megan, et al., 'Gut microbiota's effect on mental health: The gut-brain axis', *National Library of Medicine*, Vol. 7 (4), 15 September 2017, https://bit.ly/2OitjiE. Accessed on 25 June 2022.

What adversely affects gut bacteria?

1. **Processed food or junk foods** are usually loaded with sugar, devoid of healthy fibre and lack nutrients. Such foods promote the growth of bad bacteria and yeast in the gut. They can also contribute to stomach cramps and diarrhoea. Furthermore, they can compromise the barrier lining of our gut lending us open to many inflammatory diseases. Simply avoid junk and processed items.

2. **Overdoing spicy food** can cause heartburn or indigestion. Limit their use if it disturbs your system.

3. **Dairy products.** Lactose intolerance is where one lacks, or does not produce, enough of the lactase enzyme that digests the protein (lactose) in milk and other dairy products. In which case, it is best to avoid these foods or shift to lactose-free dairy products.

4. **Medications.** Excessive intake of antibiotics, anti-inflammatories, acid-blocking drugs and steroids can adversely affect the diversity and composition of gut flora and damage the gut. They can irritate the intestinal lining and may even lead to internal bleeding. Limit such medications, if you have the option.

5. **Stress.** Chronic anxiety and stress alter the central and enteric nervous systems. This can significantly impact and change the normal bacteria in the gut, even leading to a leaky gut. Cortisol released during a stress response can impede digestion and metabolism. Refer to the chapter titled 'Managing Work-Related Stress' for stress management techniques.

6. **Infections of the stomach or intestines** including bacterial
    and yeast overgrowth, and parasites can create imbalances
    in the gut microbiome. They can impair your body's ability
    to absorb nutrients, store fat and regulate blood sugar.
    These should be addressed promptly.

7. **Long-term laxative use** disturbs your gut's natural rhythm.
    Laxatives can leave you dependent on them and can deplete
    your gut flora. Try increasing your fibre intake, stay hydrated
    and get regular exercise to avoid constipation.

Addressing these factors can help prevent gut deterioration.
Now, let us discuss some ways of enhancing and making your
inner gut microbiome stronger.

What helps to restore, maintain and retain good gut health?
Regular exercise, adequate sleep and a balanced diet are the
cornerstones of good gut health. Probiotics, which are live
bacteria-rich fermented foods, such as yogurt and cheese, are
beneficial in promoting a healthy gut. Prebiotics, which are
dietary fibres found in non-digestible carbohydrates (fruits,
vegetables, etc.), are also necessary for supporting a healthy
gut biome.

For alleviating simple digestive issues, turn to natural cures
such as psyllium husk, commonly known as Isabgol in India,
for constipation; ginger, asafoetida (*hiṅg*) and carom seeds
for nausea. Chamomile tea is calming to the digestive system
and fennel seeds, used as after-meal mouth freshener, also aid
digestion. The benefits of *triphalā*—an Ayurvedic formulation—
are enormous for a healthy gut lining.

Remember that the daily health choices we make have both short-term and long-term effects. Being mindful of these will help in reviving and maintaining your digestive system.

28

Added Sugars: Poison for the Body

A small *besan* laddu (gram-flour dessert rolled into the shape of a ball), a slice of bread with jam or a simple cup of tea—they seem innocent enough, yet, they slowly poison your system. The common harmful ingredient they all have is sugar. Though it lends sweetness to our palate, sugar is bitter for our health, with myriads of ill effects. In this discussion, I am referring to 'added sugar', not the 'natural sugar' found in fruits, vegetables, grains, nuts and dairy.

The problem occurs when we consume foods laden with 'added sugars', such as mithai, cakes, cookies, sodas, tea and coffee. Even regular food items such as pasta, cereals and bread contain added sugars. Unhealthy added sugars go by the names: glucose, sucrose, maltose, dextrose, high-fructose corn syrup, molasses and cane crystals.

What is sugar and how is it made? It is a carbohydrate that provides energy to our body. The chemical name of table sugar is sucrose. It is composed of two simple sugar molecules: glucose and fructose, bound together.

Sugar is made from the juice extracted from sugar cane and sugar beet plants—as they have the greatest quantities of sucrose. The variety of sugars available are a result of variations in the manufacturing processes. The colour of the sugar depends on the molasses preserved and the chemicals added in the process. Hence, brown sugar receives its colour from the molasses it retains. In contrast, white sugar is completely stripped of molasses and bleached with chemicals.

How much sugar do we need? The natural sugars from foods are enough for our body. Fruit, dairy, vegetables and carbohydrates, all convert to glucose in the bloodstream. So, our body does not need added sugar to survive.

However, civilization has spoilt its eating habit and unnecessarily developed the sweet tooth. Hence, the American Heart Association (AHA) has a general guideline for people with normal weight. It recommends consuming no more than 9 teaspoons for men; 6 teaspoons for women; and 3–6 teaspoons for children. These are the daily maximum figures.

Added sugar you unknowingly consume. One teaspoon of added sugar is equivalent to 4 grams (about 16 calories). To give you an idea of common food items from your fridge and kitchen that are loaded with added sugar:
- 1 tablespoon of ketchup has about 1 teaspoon of sugar (4 grams)
- a 350-ml can of Coca-Cola has roughly 10 teaspoons (39 grams)
- breakfast cereal can have an upwards of 6 teaspoons of sugar per 100 grams of serving (24 grams).

Just one gulab jamun can contain up to 4.5 teaspoons of sugar. A cup of tea or coffee may contain 1–3 teaspoons of added sugar.

Multiply that by three cups a day, and you are looking at 3–9 teaspoons (12–36 grams) of sugar a day just from tea alone. We can see how easily the numbers start stacking up.

GET ME THAT DOUGHNUT FROM THE LOWEST SHELF,
I AM ON A 'LOW-SUGAR' DIET

How sugar is metabolized in the body. Sugar metabolism is the process by which the energy stored in foods that we eat is made available to us as fuel for the body. Natural and added sugars are broken down into glucose and fructose in the digestive tract before they enter the bloodstream. Both glucose and fructose are metabolized differently.

Glucose in the blood creates a 'sugar spike', which stimulates the beta cells in the pancreas to release insulin. This hormone then triggers the uptake of glucose by different cells in the body. Most of the body's cells use glucose for energy, especially the brain. Insulin also signals the liver to store any excess blood sugar as glycogen, and as lipid in the fat tissue. A few hours after a meal, your blood glucose drops or returns to base levels, and the pancreas decreases insulin production.

Unlike glucose, which is directly metabolized, fructose is first processed in the liver and then goes through the similar process above.

What happens when you consume excess added sugar? Added sugars contribute to an array of illnesses and metabolic disorders. Hence, the name 'white poison'. While the side effects of heavy sugar intake, such as weight gain, obesity and tooth decay, are obvious, there are other serious detrimental effects of sugar on the body.

Type 2 diabetes. Though obesity, genetics, lack of exercise, and the like also play a role in the development of type 2 diabetes, sugar, too, contributes to the problem. Excess consumption of sugar-laden foods and drinks causes a continual spike in blood sugar. The pancreas, overloaded with insulin production, eventually stops functioning, keeping blood sugar high. The insulin receptors in various cells of the body, too, can become less receptive or insulin-resistant, in which case, glucose levels remain elevated. This leads to prediabetes, which later progresses to type 2 diabetes.

Digestive imbalance and osteoporosis. Sugar makes the gut and blood acidic causing poor digestion and microbiome imbalance. This can lead to malabsorption of minerals and nutrients, as well as a leaky gut. Apart from that, excess sugar can put you at risk for osteoporosis and fractures.

Liver damage. The liver processes fructose found in sweetened beverages. Too much refined sugar and high-fructose corn syrup cause an accumulation of fat in the liver cells and increase the risk of non-alcoholic fatty liver disease. This is one more reason to limit foods with added sugars, like sodas and candy.

Sugar and heart health. Studies also show that excess added sugar significantly increases our risk of dying from cardiovascular disease. It increases blood pressure through sodium accumulation in the body. It lowers the good cholesterol, while raising the bad cholesterol. Further, it stops triglycerides from breaking down.

How to reduce and replace sugar in our diet. While the body tolerates a fortnightly pandering to sweets, beyond that, it is best to avoid added sugars. Fruits, vegetables, beans, nuts and whole grains, all contain natural simple sugars. The presence of fibre in them slows down the absorption of sugar and controls blood sugar more efficiently.

Also, it is best to cut back or eliminate sugar-laden beverages, sodas and desserts, as they are full of empty calories that spike your glucose levels. Where unavoidable, replace white sugar with minimally processed jaggery, honey, maple syrup or agave nectar. They also have a lower glycaemic index than white sugar, resulting in a lower and slower rise in blood glucose. However, these are also broken down into glucose in the body, and therefore, need to be consumed in moderation. And as for artificial sweeteners, shun them like the plague.

29

Benefits of Intermittent Fasting

Fasting has deep historical roots in many religious traditions and cultures around the world and is observed for both material and spiritual benefits. Fasting entails abstaining from all or some food for a certain period of time. People practise it in innumerable different ways and for various reasons.

Spiritual reasons behind fasting. It is seen by some as a technique for denying the mind and senses, thereby freeing themselves from the body's clutches. Some see it as a form of abstinence for enhancing willpower and self-control. Devotees also fast as an offering to their Lord. For example, among Hindus, fasting on the occasion of Janmashtami and Shivaratri is quite common.

Health benefits of fasting. From the perspective of physical well-being, fasting gives a break to the digestive system and downtime to the body. This helps in many ways:

- Many physiological systems get rest. They utilize the time to heal and repair. Also, food stuck to the intestinal walls gets digested. This results in cleansing of the GI tract. Various poisons get eliminated from the body, leading to detoxification.

- Limiting the calorie intake during fasting forces the body to access stored fat for energy. The burning of fat results in weight loss.

- The growth hormone secretion increases considerably, which is vital for muscle development and prevention of ageing. Several studies have linked regular fasting with longevity.[9]

- Cellular repair happens during this body downtime, which reduces the risk of cancer.

- It improves brain functioning and health. Studies in animals have shown that fasting protects against Alzheimer's and Parkinson's disease.[10]

- Research shows that fasting can help decrease inflammation levels. This is helpful in chronic conditions such as heart disease and arthritis. Bad cholesterol reduces and that is beneficial for the heart.

- The reduced intake of calories helps prevent prediabetes. However, for those who are already prediabetic and diabetic, the dips and spikes in blood sugar can be unsafe.

What happens when you fast? Whether you eat or not, your body needs energy. The liver and muscles store the energy in the

---

[9]American Heart Association News, 'Regular fasting could lead to longer, healthier life', *Heart.org*, 25 November 2019, https://bit.ly/3c7A1FG. Accessed on 8 June 2022.
[10]Lindsay Talemal, B.S., 'Caloric Intake and Its Effect on Aging and Cognitive Slowing: A Review of the Research into Intermittent Fasting', *Journal of Nutritional Medicine and Diet Care*, Volume 7, Issue 1, https://bit.ly/3xclNdv. Accessed on 8 June 2022; 'Research shows intermittent fasting may prevent Alzheimer's disease', *Alzheimer's Prevention Bulletin*, 17 February 2021, https://bit.ly/3QaBE55. Accessed on 8 June 2022.

form of glucose and release it into the bloodstream whenever the body needs it.

Fasting changes that. Eight hours into the fast, the liver exhausts the last of its glucose reserves. Then the body begins the process of gluconeogenesis. Deprived of external fuel, the body creates its own glucose mainly using fat.

If fasting is continued for several days, the body runs out of fat as well. It then enters a more serious starvation mode. The metabolism slows down, and muscles start getting burnt for energy. Muscle loss does not happen in fasts that are shorter than two days in duration.

But even these shorter fasts put your cells under mild stress. Your body responds to the challenge, strengthening its ability to deal with stress and fight disease. But in the process, the body must resort to using the stored fat for energy. This results in ketosis, which builds up acidic ketones in the blood.

Longer fasts can be unsafe. The accumulation of acid ketones can damage the liver and kidneys. Fasting also deprives you of necessary vitamins, minerals and other healthy nutrients. This can lead to fatigue, dizziness, constipation and dehydration. These dangers begin to appear when the fast stretches to a full day and more.

However, intermittent fasting mitigates most of these dangers. The limited period of the fast prevents weakness and deprivation, while retaining the benefits. Let us understand how it works.

Intermittent fasting. There are various methods of practising it. Among them, the 16/8 method is the most popular. You eat only during an eight-hour window and then fast for 16 hours. You can follow this pattern daily or for a few days of the week. Some people do not eat after 8 p.m. and have their first meal at noon. So, they miss breakfast. For others, it is easier to skip dinner.

Jagadguru Kripaluji Maharajji (Shree Maharajji) practised intermittent fasting on Mondays and Thursdays. He recommended the same for devotees as well. So, if your last meal on these two days was at 2 p.m., and you have breakfast at 8 a.m. the next day, your system gets a 16-hour rest. Having learnt it from my Guru, this is the system I follow as well.

Another popular form of intermittent fasting is where, on two days of the week, you restrict your calorie intake to 500 calories for women and 600 calories for men. The reduced calorie intake adds up over weeks to make a significant difference. This 5:2 diet is called the Fast Diet and has benefits similar to the one practised by Shree Maharajji.

Though intermittent fasting is harmless for most people, if you have medical conditions or are on medication, do consult your doctor before adopting it.

In the beginning, fasting seems difficult. You may experience hunger pangs, irritability, fatigue, headaches and insomnia. However, slowly the body adapts, and you get used to the healthy new lifestyle with its promise of a longer life.

30

Understanding and Building Immunity

Our body has an inbuilt defence mechanism for its protection. This is our immune system, which is a complex network of cells, tissues and organs protecting our body from harmful bacteria, viruses and fungi. This system quietly works in the background combating harmful invaders, and subsequently, healing and restoring good health.

When the immune system breaks down, we become susceptible to disease. Therefore, building and strengthening our body's immunity is of paramount importance. This dire need has been further heightened by the recent pandemic. It is well-nigh impossible to be vaccinated against all the mutations of Covid-19 as well as future viruses that could strike humankind. We must surely take the Covid-19 vaccine, but equally important in this uncertain scenario is to boost our own immune system through natural ways.

Let us begin by understanding how the immune system works.

Immunity is primarily of two types. We possess an innate immunity that we are born with. It includes physical barriers such as skin, mucus, saliva and tears. These keep harmful substances from entering the body. The second is acquired immunity. It is what we develop through life. When we are exposed to pathogens, the body responds by building up antibodies. The combination of these two kinds of defences is referred to as having 'immunity'.

Young children tend to fall sick more often. The reason is that they are getting exposed to many pathogens for the first time, and the immunity is still building up. By the time they reach young adulthood, the immunity is at a peak. By now, they have been exposed to various pathogens and have developed immunity to them. Besides, their body's vital energy is also at a peak. That is why they are less likely to fall sick, and when they do, they recover quickly. Older people have less vital energy in their body. This results in weakened immune systems that make them more susceptible to infections. Also, recovery period tends to be longer.

What is an immune response? Did you know that fever and sickness are often signs that the body is actively fighting off invaders? Yes, our body triggers such immune responses to repel and defend itself from hostile intruders. Let us delve into what happens in an immune response to pathogens.

Pathogens are infectious microorganisms that include bacteria, viruses, worms, fungi, protozoa and even some proteins called prions. Our immune system fights and protects us against these organisms. The first line of defence is the physical barriers discussed under innate immunity, such as our skin, mucus, saliva and stomach acid. If a pathogen gets past these barriers, it is attacked and destroyed by other parts of the immune system. These include white blood cells, bone marrow and the lymphatic system—thymus, spleen, lymph nodes and tonsils.

White blood cells are produced in the bone marrow and stored in blood and lymphatic tissues. Their role is to fight infections and destroy intruders. These specialized defender cells come to our rescue if a pathogen has gotten past our innate immune system.

White blood cells, or leukocytes, make up approximately 1 per cent of our total blood volume. They circulate throughout the body and upon detecting a pathogen, they get mobilized and begin to multiply.

These white blood cells are of two primary categories: phagocytes and lymphocytes.

- **Phagocytes.** Their role is to surround pathogens, break them down and destroy them. They are referred to as non-specific because they generate the same response to all pathogens. They are usually the first to show up by travelling to the site where there is a pathogen intrusion.

- **Lymphocytes** are more specific in their defence mechanism than phagocytes. On detecting a foreign pathogen, they start producing antibodies, which are specific to those particular pathogens.

   Once the body develops antibodies against a particular pathogen, it stores some for future protection. So, if the same antigen appears again, its specific antibodies begin to multiply and fight it off.

What is balanced or optimal immunity? We do not want an overactive or underactive immune system but an optimally balanced one. A weakened immune system can make you more prone to infections, stomach problems, slow wound healing, and the like. Immunodeficiencies can occur due to weakness, medications, illnesses like HIV, or genetics.

On the other hand, an overactive immune system is hypersensitive and overreacts to harmless substances in the environment. This is seen in eczema and asthmatic patients. When the body initiates an incorrect immune response to healthy cells, this leads to autoimmune diseases, some of which are type 1 diabetes, lupus and rheumatoid arthritis.

Both hyperimmune and hypo-immune systems are harmful. We should strive for an optimally functioning one that will ensure we are protected.

How to build your immunity. Just as every part of the body functions optimally when bolstered by healthy lifestyle habits, the immune system is no exception. We can use diet, lifestyle and psychological measures to help keep the immune system strong and working harmoniously.

Immunity-boosting diet. A balanced diet—rich in fruit and vegetables, supplemented with nuts and seeds—keeps our immune system healthy. It also promotes overall vitality and strength. Vitamins C, D and E are the most prominent vitamins for immunity. Vitamin C is found especially in citrus fruits. Vitamin D is received from sunshine. And vitamin E is received from plant-based oils. Minerals such as zinc, magnesium and selenium are also essential for maintaining our immune defences.

Drinking sufficient water keeps us hydrated and rids the body of toxins. Foods that promote healthy gut health, such as prebiotics and probiotics, also play a key role in keeping our immunity intact.

Indian spices and herbs used in cooking are known to augment immunity. These include turmeric, cloves, cinnamon, black peppercorns, cumin, garlic, ginger and onions.

Ayurvedic herbs such as *ashwagandha, gudduchi,* neem, tulsi and others are immunity-building powerhouses. *Kāḍhās* or herbal drinks made with a combination of herbs steeped in water are loaded with immune-boosting properties.

Exercise, nature and hygiene. Exercise leads to improvement in immunity markers because it increases blood flow, reduces inflammation and increases circulation of immune cells. Adopt exercises such as yoga, walking, running, swimming and pranayam if you want a robust immune system.

Also, spend time outdoors in nature, breathing in oxygen-laden morning air and soaking in the sunshine.

It goes without saying that prevention is better than cure. So, adhere to good hygiene habits like washing hands and not touching germ entry points such as eyes, nose and ears. This will prevent harmful microbes from invading the body and causing illness.

Lifestyle and attitude. Continuous or prolonged stress is the enemy of your immune system. Depressed and anxious states cause an increased production of cortisol. Escalations in cortisol have been linked to increased inflammation, decrease in lymphocytes and change in immune cell functioning. Stressed individuals also tend to sleep less, exercise less and have poor diets.

Positive thinking, meditation and humour are all stress busters. These mental habits and lifestyle adaptations go a long way in keeping the immune system healthy. I have discussed many of these topics in greater detail in other chapters of the book.

Let us be aware of this invisible protective shield built into our body by nature. If we support it with good habits and lifestyle, we will reap the benefits of strong immunity.

31

Exercise: The Magic Potion for Good Health

Do you want to enjoy a positive mindset, become more energetic, top up your health, reduce weight and push old age away? There is a magic potion for it—exercise. Its benefits are hard to overlook and available for all, irrespective of gender, age or physique. Despite this, only a small segment of people work out regularly. Surveys show that 64 per cent of people in India do not exercise.[11] There is always an excuse for avoiding it: paucity of time, social commitments, lack of motivation, fatigue or just sheer laziness.

So, if you need more motivation for regular workouts, here are some compelling reasons.

Exercise protects the quality of your life. In youth, you can do literally anything with your body and get away with it. But by the time you touch 40, your body metabolism starts slowing down, and symptoms of ageing begin raising their head. If you do not take preventive action, health begins to significantly decline in middle age. And by the time old age

---

[11]TNN, '64 per cent Indians don't exercise: Study', *The Times of India*, 3 July 2019, https://bit.ly/3NCSEPs. Accessed on 9 June 2022.

arrives, the body becomes a bag of diseases.

Hence, to maintain the quality of life you wish to lead, you must take steps to keep old age away. Among other things, pay particular attention to your muscle mass and bone density. When the former reduces, it becomes a precursor to aches, pains and joint problems. When the latter reduces, it makes you susceptible to fractures. If you have seen old people, bedridden and nursing a broken hip bone, you will understand what I mean.

Working out is a powerful counter to both these problems. It helps maintain muscle mass right into old age. It also slows the age-related loss in bone density.

Exercise prevents obesity. Like diet, physical activity plays a critical role in managing your weight. The logic is simple— when you exercise, you burn calories. To maintain your weight, you will need 150 minutes of moderate-intensity exercise every week. But if you wish to lose weight and keep it off, you will need higher amounts of exercise, along with a healthy eating plan.

Exercise can be fun. When you exercise, your brain releases certain feel-good chemicals, called endorphins. They boost your mood and you feel joyful, thereby preventing depression. If you choose to exercise through sports, dance classes, hiking, yoga or cricket, it further becomes an enjoyable social engagement with friends and relatives.

Setting up your personal exercise plan. Your body needs a judicious mix of cardio, strength training, flexibility and balance exercises. Varying the forms is a good strategy to maximize benefits. These can be broken up into sets to be covered on different days. For example, focus on the upper body on day one, the lower body on day two and cardio on day three.

Let us look at the individual components of exercise.

Cardio keeps the heart, lungs and circulatory system in good shape. Jogging, aerobics, cycling, swimming, Surya Namaskar (sun salutations), dancing, climbing stairs and brisk walking, all fall in this category.

Strength training maintains and improves muscle tone. It includes anti-gravity exercises, weightlifting and resistance training, a few times a week.

Flexibility exercises help maintain the range of motion of the joints, increase blood flow to muscles and reduce the risk of injury. Yoga is the speciality form in this category.

Balancing exercises become critical in old age as they prevent falls. Specific yogic postures help improve balance. These can also be done as often as possible.

Since each form of exercise has different benefits, a good routine should include a mix of varied forms to derive maximum benefit. Dedicate an hour every day, 5–6 days a week, for your physical workout. The 1–2 rest days will help the body rejuvenate to ensure you derive maximum value from your workouts.

32

Yoga for Physical and Mental Well-Being

As yoga studios have mushroomed around the globe, yoga has become a buzz word in the western world. Statistics reveal that one out of every seven Americans practises yoga.[12] The latest hep thing is to become a yoga teacher. What is the cause of this surge in its popularity?

Yoga bestows well-being from within. Aerobic exercises do a world of good for your heart. But they are not designed for harmonizing the flow of your prana (vital energy) or strengthening the tendons and ligaments. In contrast, yogic postures work on your cells, tissues, ligaments and organs. This understanding has led to increasing admiration for the yogic system.

Yoga tones the organs. While medical science prescribes chemicals to correct organ malfunctioning, yogic postures achieve the same without medicine. They utilize stretches, flexes and crunches to stretch and compress the bodily glands and organs. This becomes an effective technique for physically rejuvenating them.

---

[12]'Yoga: What You Need to Know', National Center for Complementary and Integrative Health, https://bit.ly/3aDCs1Y. Accessed on 9 June 2022.

Yoga renews the body, mind and spirit. In ancient Indian tradition, yoga is just one limb of a sublime practice. The word *yog* is derived from the Sanskrit word *yuj*, meaning 'to join'. Hence, the aim of yoga is to prepare us for attaining the supreme goal of union with God. Yogic postures help by bestowing physical well-being.

Simultaneously, they offer many spiritual benefits. Moving attentively—with awareness of the body and breath—develops focus. When the gentle stretching and deep breathing is integrated with meditation and relaxation, the body tension dissipates, and the nervous system relaxes. The mind, too, becomes calm, and there is an experience of renewal in spirit.

Let us see how yoga covers all domains of physical fitness and beyond.

Strength. Through yogic practice, you do not develop bulging muscles like weightlifters do. Nevertheless, you can tone up important muscle groups, which get neglected in aerobics but are essential for good health.

For example, almost 90 per cent of backaches begin when the muscles along the spine become weak. This results in vertebrae and discs moving out of place. Then more serious back problems set in. So, most back problems could be avoided with proper exercise.

Spinal muscles get neglected in aerobic exercises. However, the yogic system provides postures for strengthening the upper back like Sarpasan (snake pose) and for the lower back like Shalabhasan (locust pose).

Similarly, there are hundreds of yogic postures for a variety of important muscle groups in the body.

Flexibility. 'Use it or lose it' is a well-known phrase. One of the best ways to preserve youthfulness is to keep using the body. Flexibility is also beneficial in preventing injuries. Hence, many yogic postures focus on flexibility and suppleness through stretches, flexes, twists and turns of the body. This enhances the flow of blood and pranic energy to the cells, tissues, ligaments and organs.

As a simple example, Hasta Utthanasan (hand raising pose) in which you lift your arms over the head and bend backwards adds strength and suppleness to arms and shoulders. It also helps alleviate respiratory issues when done with synchronized breaths. The Tiryak Tadasan (swaying palm tree posture) stretches the sides of the abdomen, thereby toning the organs residing there, like the kidneys, liver, gallbladder and pancreas.

Cardio. Interestingly, yogic postures provide a super way to get cardio. Surya Namaskar, or sun salutations, is a set of 12 x 2 = 24 postures that not only covers the major organs of the body but also exercises the heart.

Modern medical research suggests that the best exercise for heart health is High-Intensity Interval Training (HIIT). In it, you exert yourself in cycles of 4–5 minutes of intense exercise, sandwiched by a small break. This can be continued for an hour.

With the help of Surya Namaskars, you can do this perfectly. Simply do one round of 12 sun salutations, followed by a few minutes of break. In this way, in an hour, aim for 60 rounds of Surya Namaskar for a perfect cardio workout.

Balance. Several asans improve balance and mental focus. These greatly help the elderly avoid falls. They include Vrikshasan (tree pose) or Dhruvasan (Dhruv's pose), Tadasan (mountain pose or palm tree pose), Garudasan (eagle pose), Anjaneyasan (low lunge pose), Utthit Hasta Padangushthasan (extended hand-to-big toe pose) and Vasishthasan (side plank pose), among others.

Inverted postures. These enhance blood circulation to the brain, which stimulates the pituitary and pineal glands. Greater blood flow is good for hair health as well. The inverted postures improve memory and are good for the eyes. They also help relieve stress by reducing the production of cortisol.

One such pose is Shirshasan or the headstand, also known as the 'king of asans'. There are others as well, such as Viparit Karani asan (legs up the wall pose), Sarvangasan (shoulder stand pose) and Halasan (plough pose).

Pranayam. Prana refers to 'the breath' and *yam* means 'to control'. Pranayam is the practice of breath regulation. Scientific studies have established that pranayam reduces stress and calms the nervous system; it is helpful in hypertension. It oxygenates the cells and release toxins from the body. It helps control diseases, such as Irritable Bowel Syndrome (IBS), asthma and allergic bronchitis.

Some of the popular pranayams are Bhastrika, Kapalbhati, Anulom Vilom, Bhramari and Ujjayi.

Therapeutic benefits. Along with keeping us healthy, yoga has also been used successfully for rehabilitation after illnesses and surgeries. However, for certain health conditions, specific postures are to be avoided. Therefore, it is advisable to learn yoga from a qualified teacher to grasp the finer nuances of the postures and their benefits.

Our Prem Yoga Academy in Dallas, Texas, USA offers a comprehensive training programme for becoming a certified yoga teacher. You will also find in-depth knowledge of yoga in my book *Yoga for the Body, Mind & Soul.*

33

Sitting Is the New Smoking: Adopt an Active Lifestyle

The modern world makes it so easy to slide into a sedentary lifestyle. The need for us to remain active has been drastically replaced by technology. We use personal vehicles to commute and appliances to do household work. And we watch TV for entertainment. Consequently, we often spend most of our day sitting.

You will be surprised to learn that the World Health Organization (WHO) places inactivity as the fourth leading risk factor for death globally. Sitting for long hours—nine hours a day or more—has been linked to diabetes, obesity, heart problems and hypertension. Not moving around slows the body's metabolism. It also increases the risk of depression. That's why the saying: 'Sitting is the new smoking.' Too much sitting damages our health in multiple ways.

Is the daily exercise regimen not enough? While exercising vigorously for about half an hour each day is important for cardiovascular health, consider this to be the basic. To stay healthy, one must remain active throughout the day. For this reason, along with exercise, coaches and health experts now give importance to Non-Exercise Activity Thermogenesis (NEAT). This is the energy spent on activities other than sleeping, eating, sports and exercise.

Let us start by looking at the easiest amongst NEATs, which is walking.

Hippocrates, father of western medicine, considered walking as man's best medicine. How right he was! Moving around or remaining active through the day has great health benefits—you remain energetic, upbeat, in shape and most importantly, add years to your life. You also get better quality sleep.

The best part is that it does not need specialized training equipment. You just need to make a few lifestyle changes. These are easy to incorporate into your daily routines once you make the resolve.

THE DOCTOR SAID I SHOULD WALK
OUR DOG TO STAY HEALTHY

Increase your number of daily steps. Studies show that to stay fit you should aim to walk at least 10,000 steps a day (about five miles). This includes steps taken for exercise and all other activities of daily living. A pedometer or Fitbit helps keep count of the steps you walk daily. It also serves as a good reminder to get up and move when you have been sitting for too long. But, even without a gadget to track us, there are other simple ways to increase the steps you walk.

Choose to walk. Add some walking to your work commute. Opt to walk or bike for short-distance errands. Park at the farthest end of the parking lot, instead of the closest. Take the stairs and avoid the elevator or the escalator—climbing stairs requires vigorous physical effort and is great for heart health. Walk when you make phone calls.

Make walking enjoyable by listening to uplifting music or discourses. That is one of the best times for self-reflection. If you prefer company, invite a friend for a walk.

Take activity breaks while working. You can take a break and walk over to a colleague's desk to talk, instead of emailing, texting or calling. You can step out of the building and have a walking meeting and get some fresh air in the process.

You will find these breaks energizing and socially uplifting. In addition, they will help to enhance your focus and concentration. If working from home, take breaks from work to attend to household chores. Or spread out your tasks through the day to break the prolonged seating mode.

You can do some stretching exercises and yoga at your desk. You can opt for a standing desk, alternating sitting and standing. Changing gears throughout the day gives you fresh packets of energy. And it helps you focus better when you return to work.

Make family time fun time. Plan fun physical activities with your family in the evenings—a game in the yard, a yoga session or just break into a dance with your children. This will do wonders for your spirits and provide you good relaxation to unwind after a long day at work.

Adopting an active lifestyle is a win-win situation. You will see your energy levels go up and your spirits uplifted. It will help you maintain your weight. And it will ward off ageing and diseases that result from a sedentary lifestyle—heart problems, diabetes and cancer.

When you consciously start to incorporate these easy-to-implement suggestions in your day, you will notice that they make a world of difference. So, get up, leave that chair and find a reason to move around!

34

Get Quality Sleep Every Night

Quality sleep is just as vital to our health as food and water. But for many of us, it takes the back seat when weighed against life's other demands. Hence, it is necessary to understand the immense benefits of a good night's rest on our overall well-being.

Why is sleep so important? Much of the body's restoration, rejuvenation and rebuilding happens during sleep. This includes functions such as hormone regulation, muscle and tissue repair, immunity enhancement, growth in children and others.

Besides providing energy and vitality to the body, quality sleep also ensures the proper working of the brain. Adequate rest improves learning by forming new pathways to assist in memory and filing of information. Good sleep helps us focus and make better decisions.

Lack of adequate sleep has been linked to heart disease, hypertension and diabetes. Sleep deprivation increases susceptibility to infections, obesity and migraine. At the emotional level, sleeping less leads to lack of focus, low performance and mood fluctuations.

How much sleep do we need in a day? The amount of rest we need varies with age and overall fitness. In general, babies need 12–16 hours. Toddlers, up to five years of age, require 10–14 hours. Children between the ages of 6 and 12 require 9–12 hours of rest. Teenagers need 8–10 hours of sleep. And adults over 18 generally require 6–8 hours of restful sleep.

Many of us do not get the recommended sleep needed to function well. If you find yourself feeling tired, lacking focus, suffering from poor performance and memory or feeling moody, you may be sleep deficient.

Here are some of the best practices for quality sleep:

Expose yourself to more bright light during the day. Your body works on the circadian rhythm, or time-keeping clock, which is synced with the sunrise and sunset. Natural sunlight keeps this rhythm healthy and improves sleep quality and duration. Studies have shown that daytime light exposure reduces the time it takes to sleep and improves sleep efficiency.[13]

Sleep and wake up at consistent times. Irregular sleep patterns can also alter your circadian rhythm and levels of melatonin which signals your brain to sleep. Going to bed at the same time and waking up on time daily, including the weekends, can enhance sleep quality.

Eliminate blue light exposure in the evening. Night-time light exposure disrupts the circadian rhythm by tricking the brain into thinking it is still daytime and signals it to stay awake. This

[13]Mawer, Rudy, '17 Proven Tips to Sleep Better at Night', *Healthline.com*, 28 February 2020, https://bit.ly/2HuJTW6. Accessed on 25 June 2022.

reduces the release of melatonin, which is the hormone needed to relax and get deep sleep. So, put away the smartphones and computers, and do not watch TV before bed. Refraining from social media and news will reduce stimulation to the mind and help it unwind.

Get regular exercise. A daily routine of physical exercise enhances all aspects of sleep. This will also tire you for a good night's sleep.

Relax your mind in the evening and night. Relaxation techniques are highly effective in improving sleep quality and are simple to do. Read a good book, listen to light music or take a hot shower. The body and mind both start to wind down for the day.

Try meditation. Before sleeping, sit in your bed for five minutes and meditate. Bring the image of God into the temple of your mind. It will spiritualize your consciousness even during sleep. In addition, subtle body relaxation is a powerful technique for deep healing. You can learn about it in *Yoga for the Body, Mind & Soul.*

Avoid caffeine late in the day. It is a stimulant and can remain in the blood for 6–10 hours. Caffeine products such as tea, coffee and soda, to name a few, consumed late in the day stimulate the nervous system and prevent your body from relaxing at night. Instead, drinking herbal teas, such as chamomile and lavender, calm the brain and help invoke deep, restful sleep.

Sip warm milk and honey before bedtime. Milk contains the hormone tryptophan, which is a precursor to serotonin.

Serotonin is a neurotransmitter that works as a natural sedative in the brain. The calcium in milk also helps relax the muscles of the body. Combined with a carbohydrate such as honey, serotonin is transmitted to the brain faster, enabling you to fall asleep quickly and stay asleep longer.

Rule out any sleep disorders or problems. Sometimes an underlying health condition may be causing disruptions to your sleep. Conditions such as sleep apnoea, insomnia and sleep movement disorders need to be assessed and treated. If you constantly struggle with sleep despite trying holistic practices, do not ignore it. Consult your medical healthcare provider.

The Vedas inform us that the highest bliss one can experience in the material realm is during deep sleep. If we want that bliss every night, we must pay attention to our lifestyle choices. The recommendations outlined in this chapter will help you feel well-rested, energized and ready to take on the day.

35

Build a Powerful Morning Routine

To conquer the day, you must claim the morning. Tim Cook, CEO of Apple, Indra Nooyi, former PepsiCo CEO, Michelle Obama, former US First Lady and numerous other accomplished people rise early, while most are still asleep. They take advantage of minimal distractions, enhanced creativity and a tranquil state of mind that are dominant in early morning hours. This gives them the edge and momentum to become peak performers. In this manner, the one who conquers the morning achieves success giving credibility to the old adage, 'The early bird catches the worm.'

The morning hours are sublime. These magical hours are roughly from 4 a.m. to 6 a.m. The Vedas refer to this period as the *Brahma Muhūrt,* or the Creator's time. It is the best time for quality focused work. The environment is undisturbed, the atmosphere has high levels of prana and the mind is poised. It is the ideal time to fix your mind on God with least effort. That is why sages, rishis and *sādhaks* (spiritual aspirants) invariably wake up well before dawn to take advantage of the magical hours.

Higher states become accessible to the brain. During the day, beta brainwaves dominate. But in the morning, one naturally goes into the alpha or theta states. These frequencies are conducive to creativity and learning. Writers, painters and singers utilize this time for their creative ideas and for perfecting their work. Focus and flow are naturally escalated due to lack of environmental disturbances.

Why early risers are few. Though early morning is full of potential, most people fail to utilize it. The average waking up time is about 7 a.m. Lack of awareness of its benefits is one reason. Detrimental lifestyle habits are the other.

About 150 years ago, there was no electricity in people's homes. So, after sunset, there was not much to do—people slept early and naturally woke up early. Fast forward to the twenty-first century. Now late-night activities dominate the lifestyle. And once the ideal sleep threshold is passed, one can stay awake for hours. Slowly, one falls into a habitual pattern of late-night sleeping and waking up late.

However, as is with most habits, with practise, we can inculcate the discipline of rising early. And with sustained effort, it can be mastered. Here are some powerful ways to reclaim your mornings and move ahead in life.

A successful morning starts the night before. Our brain secretes the sleep-inducing chemical melatonin, between 10 and 11 in the evening. You can take advantage of that by sleeping early. When you make a habit of it, melatonin secretion at that time will automatically increase, making it easier for you to sleep between those hours.

Quality of sleep is equally important to ensure productive mornings. For sound sleep, have a light dinner, completing it at least three hours before bedtime. This allows for proper digestion and prepares you for relaxing sleep.

Before dozing off, take time to introspect and engage in some quiet moments of prayer and gratitude. These handful of practices will help you get deep sleep and wake up refreshed and inspired.

The morning routine. The first two waking hours of the day are prime because they kick-start and set the day for success. Learn to harness the power of solitude available at this time. Avoid the urge to pick up the mobile to check the latest messages or social media posts.

Instead, make your mornings effective by incorporating exercise, contemplation and time for personal growth. Here is a sample morning schedule for you.

Dedicate an hour for physical exercise. Fitness ensures that you have a surging supply of energy and stamina to accomplish all the tasks of the day. Exercising first thing in the morning releases the happy hormone, serotonin. It also gives a sense of accomplishment.

Invest an hour on personal development. Successful people realize that **inner victories lead to external excellence.** Many people utilize this hour by journaling about their goals, which gives them clarity and focus. Others read meaningful books or watch inspiring videos to learn and train in their subject of interest. It can be a time for reflection on values you strive to instill. Essentially, this is your time to build character and pursue personal growth.

For those inclined to spiritual practice, I have detailed the **KripaluPadhati** method earlier in the book that you can engage in for an hour. It includes meditation, listening to divine knowledge, prayer and more. It will fire you up to take on challenges of the day effortlessly.

Put it to practice. If you are a late riser, you cannot suddenly change things around. Start chipping away 15 minutes from your sleep every month, until you reach your desirable morning wake-up time. This will allow your body to slowly return to its natural circadian rhythm that was disrupted due to a poor lifestyle. You will become an early sleeper and riser, with the benefit of quality sleep. You can then invest those two morning hours in your physical well-being, emotional health and spirituality, to live the best days of your life.

36

Laughter: The Best Medicine

A good hearty laugh does wonders. It is like an energy booster that lightens our burdens and lifts our spirits. In difficult social interactions, it is an instant tension diffuser. But that is not all. The simple act of laughing has several health benefits.

Many saints had jovial natures, full of mirthfulness and humour. Their playful and childlike demeanour added to the charisma of their personality. Ramakrishna Paramahansa and his illustrious disciple Swami Vivekananda were renowned for their jocose temperament. Saint Kabir used wit to teach divine wisdom. Jagadguru Kripaluji Maharaj was famous for his *uccha attahās* (outburst of loud laughter). He had a tremendous sense of humour and would keep people around him regaled with a constant stream of light-hearted comments and jokes.

Emotional benefits of laughter. It is cathartic; a burst of laughter is like a release of steam from a pressure cooker. It wipes off worries and stresses from your mind, to start afresh. Or rather, it brings the balance back in your body and mind.

Gelotology is the study of laughter and its effects on the body. When we laugh, 15 facial muscles contract. The good news is that spontaneous and induced laughter both have similar benefits. That means, even if you force yourself to laugh, you will get the same benefits as from naturally arising laughter.

What medical science says. The physical act of laughing results in chemical changes in the body. Laughter releases endorphins, the feel-good chemicals in the brain. They lower blood pressure and the risk of a heart attack. The light-hearted feeling triggers the release of neuropeptides which help fight stress and prevent future illnesses. Also, the limbic system gets stimulated, which boosts body immunity. There is an increase in the production of antibodies and T cells to fight off disease.

Laughing counters depression. In 2015, the WHO estimated that 300 million people in the world, i.e. 4.3 per cent of the world's population, suffer from depression. It is a major cause of disability, sometimes even leading to suicide. Given this scenario, it will not be surprising if in the future, we see prescriptions, like:

Rx Laughter five times a day (spontaneous or induced).

Increase dose if needed. No side effects.

Refills: No limit.

Laughter alone is not the cure for serious mental ailments. Yet, small doses of it added over time can go a long way in lifting the veil of gloom and engendering mental well-being. Here, it is also necessary to mention that excessive laughter, or ill-timed laughter, can be a sign of mental health conditions.

Social benefits of laughter. It helps break the ice and strengthens social bonds. As the saying goes, 'Laugh and the world laughs with you, cry and you cry alone.' Well-chosen and well-timed mirth helps cope with difficult situations. It makes people let go of anger, resentment, hurt and grudges.

How to laugh more. Statistics reveal that adults laugh 15–20 times on average. Children laugh three times more. And babies laugh about 300 times a day.

Living life is a serious business. But every now then, it is important to take little breaks from it. Here are some suggestions on how to do it.

Learn to see the humour in everyday situations. A spontaneous burst of laughter or even a planned laugh will win many hearts. Many times, it does not take much—a simple joke, an expression or a funny remark can lead to an instant eruption of laughter. Gradually, this will become a habit. Then joviality and cheerfulness will come naturally to you. Although laughing at others is no laughing matter, learning to laugh at yourself will take you a step further in making light of difficult life situations.

But what to do if you still cannot laugh? Start practising with a smile. It is the beginning of laughter.

Try to incorporate a hasyasan in your exercise or yoga routine. If living in India, you must have seen the laughter clubs that meet in the mornings in parks. In the JKYog workshops on yoga and meditation, participants engage in four kinds of laughter:

- Attahas hasyasan: lifting hands and laughing loudly.
- Dandiya hasyasan: clapping on either side and laughing.
- Gur-gur hasyasan: laughing with lips closed.

- Gud-gud hasyasan (done in pairs): tickling each other on the waist to evoke laughter.

Make room for laughter. Believe me, a good belly laugh, now and then will do wonders for you, and also for those around you. I highly recommend that you add it to your life's toolkit. And above all, it is free. It does not cost anything!

37

Keep Old Age Away with a Healthy Heart

Heart disease is the number-one killer in the world. Globally, one in three people dies because of cardiovascular diseases (CVDs). This is a term collectively used for all kinds of heart ailments—including high blood pressure, clogged arteries, valve dysfunctions, stroke and arrhythmia (irregular heartbeat). With 28 per cent of deaths attributed to heart disease,[14] India is now the heart disease capital of the world. What is even more alarming is that the onset of the disease is occurring 6–10 years earlier in Indians. And the fatality rates are much higher. Heart disease is a silent epidemic, and the first warning sign is unfortunately very often a heart attack.

These are alarming statistics. But what makes Indians more predisposed to getting heart disease? Studies indicate a genetic predisposition amongst the Indian population. A host of behavioural risk factors are also at play here. A diet that has fewer fruits and vegetables, high saturated fats, and highly processed grains. Low physical activity. High stress levels and use of tobacco, all are conducive to poor heart health. Together

---

[14]Parveen, Rahiba R., 'There's a 50% rise in heart diseases in India. Blame salt, sugar and air pollution', *The Print*, 13 September 2018, https://bit.ly/3ySjoFR. Accessed on 15 June 2022.

these result in high blood pressure, raised blood lipids, elevated sugar levels and obesity.

Why our heart is so important. Though it is about the size of your fist, the heart provides blood to each part of the body, even to itself. It never rests, not even for a moment. It never complains, unlike other muscles when they get tired. But when it finally decides to rest, it brings an end to life. Therefore, it deserves much more attention than what many people give it.

Our heart is the most vital organ of the circulatory system. The blood pumped by it delivers oxygen and nutrients to the cells of the body. While returning, it carries the waste products. Any disruption to this blood flow cycle leads to shortness of breath, numbness and tingling in the hands and feet, muscle cramps, pains, and the like. Improper blood flow to the brain due to narrowing of blood vessels as we age causes dementia.

An unhealthy heart can create lots of problems. But the good news is that many of these behavioural risk factors can be managed. Medical treatments can control cholesterol, hypertension and diabetes. But more important is making heart-healthy lifestyle choices. An ounce of prevention is worth a pound of cure.

All these lifestyle choices—diet, exercise and an active lifestyle—are discussed in much greater detail in several chapters of this book. Here, we list some key aspects related to heart health that are helpful to bear in mind.

Cardio exercises are most beneficial. During aerobic activity, the heart pumps faster and deeper to supply a greater amount of oxygen to the working muscles. When practised regularly, this increases the capacity of the heart to pump out more blood per beat, which improves its efficiency and reduces the resting heart rate. Your resting heart rate, which should ideally be between 65 and 80 beats per minute, is often an indicator of heart health. The lower it is, the stronger the heart.

Thirty minutes of moderate-intensity exercise is recommended five times a week. Moderate means that your breathing quickens, but you are not out of breath. You can converse comfortably but not sing. When not motivated to exercise, remind yourself that physical inactivity is one of the biggest risk factors for coronary heart disease.

Trim your waist. As a general guide, a waist measurement of above 32 inches for women and above 36 inches for men is an indication that you are in the high-risk category. Unfortunately, Asian populations seem to have a genetic predisposition to abdominal obesity and need to make greater efforts in keeping the belly fat off. Try Pada Utthanasan (lifting legs while lying on the back pose), Pada Vrittasan (feet-circling pose), Pada Sanchalanasan (cycling pose) and sit-ups.

Men are more prone to heart diseases. They tend to get heart attacks at younger ages. However, heart diseases in women show up after menopause when the oestrogen levels drop. The symptoms they manifest are different from men.

Watch these numbers as they are the best predictors of your heart health. Maintain cholesterol, blood pressure, Body Mass Index (BMI) and blood glucose levels in the permitted range.

Smoking or use of tobacco ranks high as one of the risk factors for developing heart disease. Exposure to second-hand smoke is also equally harmful. It is best to abstain from smoking and alcohol. Period.

Meditation will alter your mental chemistry to bring calm. At the same time, it will help you purify your spiritual heart. While this material heart is of one lifetime, the spiritual heart will remain with you for endless lifetimes.

Reduce your stress levels. When you are overcome with stress, remind yourself of the message of Shree Krishna from the Bhagavad Gita:

karmaṇy-evādhikāras te mā phaleṣhu kadāchana   (2.47)

'Put in your best effort and leave the results to God.' Your worrying and stress will not change the outcomes.

Ensure that you take good care of your heart for a long, healthy and spiritually enriched life.

Section Three

....

HARMONY IN RELATIONSHIPS

38

Relationships Enrich Your Life

If I ask you, 'What possession is most important for a long and happy life?' you would most likely list money, fame, status, health, and so forth. But what if I say there is something else, which has an even more profound effect? You would probably think I am exaggerating, but I am not. It is backed by one of the longest-running studies that has spanned over eight decades.

The study of adult development at Harvard Medical School. *In 1938, scientists at Harvard started a study tracking the lives of 268 sophomores of the Ivy League university.[15] A few years later, they started another parallel study with a group of 456 youth in poor and disadvantaged areas of Boston. Since then, the researchers followed the lives of these participants, recording their successes and failures.*

Some participants became lawyers, businessmen and doctors. One of the original participants even became the US president. This was none other than John F. Kennedy. However, not every participant had a successful life. A few even turned out to be schizophrenics or alçoholics.

What did the research reveal as the most important trait predicting longevity? Happy relationships. The study showed that people who are more socially connected to family, friends

---

[15]Mineo, Liz, 'Good genes are nice, but joy is better', *The Harvard Gazette*, 11 April 2017, https://bit.ly/3NRzEwY. Accessed on 14 June 2022.

and community are happier, healthier and live longer lives than people who are less connected.

The researchers noted that IQ made only a small difference in the salaries of the participants. However, people who had 'warm relationships' progressively reached higher salaries. Respondents who had warm childhood relationships earned significantly more than others who had bitter ones.

Yet, today, with our fast-paced lifestyle, we easily overlook our relationships. Most people hardly work towards building healthy connections. Very often, they are busy running after the next promotion, a larger house or a bigger car. In the process, they neglect this important dimension of the human experience.

People spend several hours in the gym to keep themselves fit. While physical exercise is undeniably important, the Harvard study revealed that healthy relationships are an even better determinant of health. People who had loving company felt less physical pain and had better mental health in their old age.

The Harvard study concluded that while maintaining good relationship had several advantages, the opposite was also true. Other than alcohol and smoking, loneliness was found to be a major factor leading to poor mental and physical health in later life. That was because the experience of loneliness proved toxic. People who were more isolated than they desired, were more unhappy, their health and brain function declined sooner in life, and they lived shorter lives than people who were not lonely. Further, it was not just the number of connections one had, but the quality of the close relationships that mattered.

What science has proven in its study of over eight decades, India has been following for centuries. This is why, community activities find such an important place in Indian society. No wonder then that most Indians believe it takes a village to raise a child!

However, relationships are messy and complicated. Nurturing them requires a lot of time and effort. The subsequent chapters of this section will guide you on how to build healthy and sustainable relationships for a happy and long life.

39

Communicate Effectively

Our relationships get nurtured through sound and effective communication. More than mere exchange of information, effective communication is about conveying ideas, motivating and influencing people. It is about understanding others and being understood.

Your speech is an expression of your thoughts and sentiments. If you can articulate your thoughts well, you can cultivate healthy relationships and diplomatically navigate conflicts.

Communication involves a sender, a receiver and a message. The sender transforms thoughts into communicable messages and the receiver interprets them. This exchange could be between two people, a small group or a large audience. While this model seems flawless, it is never so—messages are often misinterpreted, misunderstood or distorted in delivery. That is why we need to master the art of communication.

Here are some ways of improving your language skills for healthier relationships.

Adopt a positive tone for all communication. Whether it is a quick dialogue or a serious discussion, the style should be warm and constructive. What you say and how you say creates the communication 'climate'. People are more inclined to share information and speak openly if they feel comfortable talking to you.

Be empathetic.

Suppose you visit a shoe shop to purchase a pair for yourself. The shopkeeper shows you a pair. You try them on and then tell him, 'They are too small. My feet do not even go into these.'

'How can that be?' the shopkeeper responds. 'They fit me fine.'

'They may fit you well,' you say to him. 'But I need a pair for my feet, not yours.'

What mistake is the shopkeeper making here? He believes shoes that perfectly fit him should also fit others equally well. Isn't that ridiculous? But this is the same mistake we often make while communicating. The employer tells his employees they should be more motivated. Parents tell their children to prioritize studies. They repeat it over and over. And yet, the communication fails to have the desired results because the other party has its own perspective, which was completely neglected. It is just like the shopkeeper repeatedly saying, 'This shoe fits me well; it must fit you too.'

Thus, the dictum: 'Put yourselves in others' shoes.' This is the quality of empathy, which is the foundation of good communication.

Do not accuse, criticize or ridicule. When others do not meet expectations or make a mistake, it is human nature to criticize. We do this with the intention that the other will improve the erring behaviour. But it does not help. On the contrary, it creates an adversarial environment and becomes counterproductive. Instead, being supportive and gentle allows the other to open up. This facilitates an authentic conversation.

Be keen and show genuine concern. Use uplifting language when others share good news and encourage them further. Use supportive and caring words when discussing adverse situations.

Watch your tone and volume. Your voice and its intensity are cues to the quality of your conversation. Make sure you express your interest by being audible. But do not be loud or belligerent. Emphasize your words where needed by changing the tone of your voice. You can liken this to a period (full stop) versus an exclamation mark while writing.

Keep a solution-oriented mindset. Conversations can be made disheartening by focusing on problems instead of solutions. Negative people add fuel to the fire by focusing on differences of opinion. This inflames an already tense situation. Instead, go in with the attitude of arriving at a solution by establishing common ground. It will enable you to influence others constructively.

Be willing to compromise and apologize. Remember that it is better to be kind than to be right. To maintain harmony in relationships, your ability to compromise and adjust is a valuable trait. Approach every conversation with the intention of preserving peace and supporting the other. This will make you flexible in your thoughts and actions.

Do not multitask while listening. Make it a habit to not fidget, read emails or send messages during face-to-face interactions. Keep smartphones, laptops and other distractions away during any discussions. This will allow you to be an engaged listener.

We have discussed the beneficial attitudes to adopt while communicating in relationships. These will make you more constructive in your dealings with others. Now, let us look at techniques to adopt that will make conversations fruitful.

Listen with attention. Listening is one of the most important communication skills. God has given us two ears and only one mouth, so that we may listen more and talk less. However, people are so eager to speak that they remain distracted while listening. Consequently, they focus on what they would like to say when the other stops speaking.

We should listen to understand rather than to respond. This means to actively focus on both—the verbal and non-verbal aspects of the conversation.

Allow the other person to finish. Train yourself to respond only after others have completed their conversation. Do not interrupt by saying things like, 'If you think that is bad, let me tell you what happened to me.' When you prevent someone from sharing their thoughts, you indicate that their views are not as important as yours.

In conflicts, be mindful to not veer off topic. Simple discussions can often escalate and turn into arguments by mentioning past hurts. It is best to focus on the present issue and facts related to that alone. Draw boundaries related to the topic(s) being discussed.

If the discussion gets excessively heated, exit the dispute gracefully by simply saying, 'I think this is important for us. Can we return to it when we both have more clarity?'

Do not talk unless it improves the silence. Remember, silence is golden. When uncertain of the topic, do not feel the need to converse to fill up the awkward silence. If you do not have anything meaningful to contribute to the conversation, keeping quiet is a good stance to take. You will see that, sooner or later, someone will speak up and fill the silence.

Further, when in a group, allow a healthy silence to give everyone a window of opportunity to step into the conversation. For example, instead of dominating the dinner table dialogue, stay quiet and allow others to contribute. This will provide equal space for everyone to be heard.

Non-verbal communication. Beyond conventional speech, your non-verbal cues, such as gestures, body language and facial expressions, are also powerful means of communicating your feelings and thoughts. They can be interpreted standalone or make your speech more emphatic. For example, simple things like a smile or a frown convey your approval or disapproval within a conversation. The same goes for a nod, a pat on the back, the distance apart, your posture, and so forth.

While non-verbal communication varies based on culture, generation and gender, some cues are universal. Here are some common ones:
- Maintaining eye contact with the person you are talking to expresses your interest in the conversation.

– Standing with arms crossed suggests feeling defensive or closed off.

– Sitting or standing at the other's level while communicating shows respect.

– The tone of your voice also reveals your enthusiasm or lack thereof.

Effective communication is essential for maintaining good relationships. Like any other skill such as singing or dancing, good communication requires consistent practise. You can upgrade your skills by trying the tips shared in this chapter.

40

Your Relationship Bank Account

Human relationships are delicate matters. They are subject to the vagaries of human nature—mood swings, ego, selfishness, envy, and the like. As a result, they are fragile and need to be nurtured carefully. This chapter teaches you how to prevent them from getting derailed.

Think of a relationship as a bank account. The bank allows you to make deposits and withdrawals. However, withdrawals are limited to the extent you have deposited. Anything beyond it goes into overdraw mode. The same concept can be applied to relationships.

What are the deposits in relationships? These are the loving gestures, affection, making adjustments, keeping a helping attitude and taking the humble position, to name a few. Every time we smile at another, keep a commitment or are supportive, we make meaningful deposits. Extending a helping hand and complimenting, all go a long way to build a beautiful and lasting bond.

What do withdrawals look like? They are the negative and unpleasant interactions we initiate. Chiding the other, pointing out a fault or asking for an inconvenient favour are some of the ways by which we deplete our relational deposits.

Ideally, relationships should flow with affectionate feelings and positive interactions. These may be interspersed with a few displeasing moments that become necessary or unavoidable. In a healthy relationship, deposits should far exceed the withdrawals.

The Golden Ratio. *A study on marriage was conducted by relationship researcher, John Gottman at the University of Washington.[16] He allowed couples to fill out questionnaires and spend the weekend in an apartment hooked up with multiple cameras. After their participation, he followed the married couples for several years to see who stayed together happily or unhappily, and who divorced.*

He discovered a magic ratio of 5:1. What does that mean? The ratio of positive interactions to negative interactions had to be greater than 5:1 for couples to stay happily together.

Hence, favourable deposits are essential. Unfortunately, that is what we often neglect. We take others for granted and forget to express our affection and gratitude. In the meantime, withdrawals keep happening, and the relationship goes into overdraw mode.

This is very commonly observed in married couples. Newly-weds shower immense care and affection on their spouse. Initially, the deposits keep pouring in. They team up to work

---

[16]Dixon, Travis, 'Studying Marriage: Gottman's Love Lab and the Four Horsemen of Divorce', *IB Psychology*, 9 May 2009, https://bit.ly/3PhjRYD. Accessed on 25 June 2022.

together on house chores at the beginning of their married life. But as the years pass by, they take the relationship as a given.

Soon enough, the nagging comments, inconsiderate behaviours and demands for time become the norm. Simultaneously, pleasant interactions become an infrequent occurrence. The relationship then goes on the rocks. The husband and wife are puzzled why something that had a fairy-tale beginning is now so frustrating.

Why children rebel. The same can happen between parents and children if the relationship is not handled carefully. It is a bond of care, trust and innumerable loving exchanges. But to raise capable children, parents have to strike a balance between being soft and stern.

Parental duties include guiding children away from detrimental activities, pointing out their mistakes and even reprimanding them. Though well-intended and a necessary part of parenthood, these classify as withdrawals from the parent-child bank account.

If these withdrawals subsist without adequate deposits, children become rebellious and uncontrollable. The child exclaims, 'I do not have to listen to you!' If you observe such behaviour, it is safe to assume that your relationship account has been depleted.

If your child refuses to understand your legitimate rationale, it may be a signal that you need to replenish your visible deposits. This can be done by actively listening to your children's problems, appreciating their work and providing support. These gestures can have a magical effect in nullifying the negative side effects of pointing out faults in your child.

Tactfully handle challenging situations at work. Workplace dynamics are ever-changing and evolving. It is critical to know how to handle difficult situations like pointing out a subordinate's fault. Management experts recommend positioning criticism between layers of compliments. This is sometimes referred to as the 'sandwich method'.

Another technique that works well is, while pointing a mistake, give a suggestion on how to fix it. The other person can then either accept or reject the suggestion. This method is subtle and provides a chance for improvement.

Realize that relationships require effort. Do you remember the last time you complimented your spouse? How often did you spend one-on-one exclusive time with your children? When was the last time you appreciated your relative or co-worker? Remember the 5:1 ratio before you pull them up for their mistakes.

Build the relationship accounts by enhancing the deposits. Adorn your interactions with praise, smiles and genuine concern. Doing so will reduce the strain and make your relationships robust. It will allow for unpleasant withdrawals to be absorbed without any damage. This is the emotional bank account formula for successful relationships.

41

Expectations Ruin Relationships

One common culprit in the downfall of healthy relationships is our own expectations. We expect others' views to match ours, and that they should do as we expect. When those expectations are unfulfilled, we feel we have been wronged and become upset.

This trend can be observed across all kinds of relationships: parent-child, siblings, friends, husband-wife, and so forth.

- *I am upset because my family did not greet me lovingly after a hard day's work. I had expected they would be more caring.*
- *I am annoyed because my child did not get the grades I had hoped she would.*
- *I am mad because my spouse does not understand my sensitive nature.*

These are all examples of unfulfilled expectations. If they were met, we would be happy with the other party. But the moment they are not, conflict arises.

Some expectations are reasonable, such as fulfilling job responsibilities at work, non-violence in our interactions and honesty in dealings. More often, however, anticipations are unrealistic and unnecessarily jeopardize relationships.

To avoid upsetting the apple cart, here are a few tips and some mistakes to watch out for.

People are not mind-readers. We often presume that our thoughts and values will be obvious to others.

For example, you see that the trash is full. You expect a family member to take it out while you look after other responsibilities. The trash remains intact, and you feel offended. You give them a piece of your mind.

The family is surprised at your reaction, as they were not aware of your intention. They too become upset.

The situation could have been easily avoided. You could have asked your family to help take out the trash, instead of simply assuming they would. Remember, others may have the best intention, but if they do not know what you are expecting, then their chance of fulfilling it is dim.

Expectations cannot be met all the time. The wife expects the husband home at 6 p.m. every day, whereas the boss needs him to work till 8 p.m. today. The dilemma before the poor fellow is whose expectations should he fulfil? Staying back at work will make the wife unhappy and leaving early will put his job at risk.

So, do remember that expectations cannot always be fulfilled.

Hold others to gentler standards. We all are different in our experiences, *sanskārs* (accumulated past tendencies), beliefs and values.

For example, you may define cleanliness as a spotless home for which you toil daily. But your family members may feel that cleaning once a week is sufficient.

Another example is the frequency of communication. You send 10 messages to someone to ensure alignment and only get one in return. That may be perfectly normal for the other party. Yet, you feel hurt because you view it as callousness.

Because of such diversity, it is unrealistic to impose your standards on others. While it is good to set high standards for yourself, you cannot hold others to the same. Each person has their own set of skills and capabilities, which will invariably differ from yours. Leniency and understanding will result in less disappointments.

Respect opposing views. Often, we make the mistake of wanting others' likes and dislikes to match ours. If we like tea, our spouse should enjoy it too. If we like to read, our child should also relish the same. If we like attending satsang, our family members should also love it.

Now change this. Instead of arguing about others' opinions, respect their freedom to hold a different perspective. While maintaining your own view, be respectful and accepting of others.

The root cause of expectations is selfishness. Expectations are based upon 'I want' and 'I need'. They are rooted in the attitude: 'What's in it for me?'

You may feel that some of your expectations are truly for the welfare of the other. You may even declare that you are offering selfless service, yet, in reality, the selfishness exists, albeit covertly.

A new member joined our temple congregation in Dallas. He came to me after three months, and said, 'Swamiji, the devotees here are so ungrateful.'

I asked him, 'What did they do?'

'I served the community so selflessly. I went out of my way to offer services that were needed,' he said. 'But I did not get the appreciation I was looking for.'

I said to him, 'If you were seeking tons of appreciation, then how were you selfless?'

If our expectations are genuinely for the sake of others, the test is that we will be more accepting of reality. We will be flexible in our attitudes and sacrificing in our dealings and not get upset upon their unfulfillment.

Hence, for your relationship dynamics to be positive, learn to be more selfless. This is expressed in the form of sacrifice, understanding, tolerance and acceptance.

42

Overcome Fault-Finding

Finding faults in others, playing the blame game and judging people are personality traits that need no introduction. We all are guilty of them, to a lesser or greater extent. Factually, fault-finding is the easiest of things. It needs no intelligence or integrity of character, as this story illustrates.

A professor handed out surprise test papers. With tepidity, the students received their question sheets. To their surprise, all they saw was a crisp blank paper with a black dot in the centre.

The professor asked the students to write about what they saw. Then, he read out their responses. All of them, without exception, wrote about the black dot—its position, size, etc.

The black dot had grabbed the attention of the students, not the spotless white space that filled most of the paper. The teacher then explained that he was not grading them for it—he simply meant to teach them an important lesson.

We too are quick to notice people's imperfections but slow to observe the good. This tendency of being critical or judgemental runs deep. Why is it so pervasive?

Its root cause is the ego within. It is said: 'Pride is the mask of one's own faults.' Our mind loves to bolster itself by diminishing the value of others. It justifies itself by thinking: 'Since they have defects, they are wrong. I am better than them, so I am right.' The ego experiences a perverse happiness by nourishing itself in this manner. And this quickly becomes an intoxication.

Judgements are often ill-informed. Sometimes we pass judgement or make impressions without knowing the other person's full story. Instead, if we delve into their background, we may discover that they are really not what we thought.

Ian Maclaren, a nineteenth-century author, expressed it well: 'Be kind, for everyone you meet is fighting a hard battle.' People go through their unique experiences and hardships in life, which make them what they are today. If we keep this in mind, it will help develop empathy and compassion.

Judging people is easy; loving them is difficult. Love means accepting the other, with both their flaws and virtues, without needing them to change. That is why it is said, 'Hate the sin, not the sinner.'

So, even if you have an obstinate spouse or a difficult mother-in-law, you can choose to overlook the differences and learn to enjoy their company. In doing so, you will see positivity slowly replace bitterness.

Our mind often tricks us into believing we need others to change for their good. But, invariably, our own discomfort with the present state is the motive behind it. Apply this test to yourself. When you ask others to change, but they don't, do you become angry? If so, it is a sure-shot indication that your motive was selfish.

Check yourself—are you overly critical of everything? Are you habituated to seeing the shortcomings in your surroundings? Do you feel as if the whole world is wrong, and you are right? If so, you need to stand back and examine whether the shortcoming is in you.

If our mind is heavily focused on the shortcomings of our family members, the defects of the boss and the meanness of relatives, it is highly likely that our mindset is faulty because of which the world appears defective.

In this case, correct yourself. Transform from being a negative thinker to a positive one. Focus on solutions rather than the problems. Develop the habit of noticing the inspiring and noble qualities of others.

Fault-finding harms you. Yes, you do yourself a disservice by pointing out the blemishes of others. Thinking, 'He has this defect', 'She has that flaw', 'They are so negative', and so on results in focusing your mind on others' shortcomings. Such negative *chintan* makes our already impure mind more impure.

Remember that God is seated within everyone. Hence, practise seeing the divinity in all. This attitude is the highest. But if you cannot bring yourself to see God in everyone, then at least learn not to see the bad in them.

Look at your own faults. The urge to find faults in others arises from the impurity of our own mind. The nature of the polluted mind is to gravitate to others' weaknesses. And when we do so, we stop looking at our own shortcomings; our own self-improvement gets neglected. Consequently, our own defects keep increasing.

The most effective solution to overcome this tendency is to examine your own shortcomings. Through introspection and reflection, scrutinize your thoughts, words and actions. Then, carefully weed out whatever is defective. You will grow in virtue and also become more peaceful in the process.

43

Anger Spoils It All

Anger can be one of the most destructive emotions. When it strikes, it disturbs our inner peace and destroys our ability to think rationally. A lifetime of wisdom and good manners vanish in one wave of anger, only to leave us regretful later. History and our own experience are proof of the damage anger causes to relationships and humanity.

Anger has detrimental effects on our body and mind. Though rage varies in intensity from mild irritation to intense fury, in all cases, it prompts physiological changes in the body. The brain triggers the release of stress hormones—adrenaline and cortisol. Consequently, blood pressure and body temperature increase. If this happens once in a while, the body makes up for it. But if anger visits regularly, it can lead to headaches, digestive problems, insomnia, high blood pressure and eczema, to name just a few disorders.

Getting angry frequently is a bigger predictor of early death due to heart disease than smoking, eating junk food and lack of exercise put together. Even recalling times when you felt truly furious can be perilously harmful for the heart and overall health.

The Vedic scriptures classify anger as a *mānas rog* (mental affliction). The Bhagavad Gita describes its consequences in the severest terms:

krodhād bhavati sammohaḥ sammohāt smṛiti-vibhramaḥ
smṛiti-bhranśhād buddhi-nāśho buddhi-nāśhāt praṇaśhyati

(2.63)

'Anger leads to clouding of judgement, and that results in bewilderment of memory. When memory is bewildered, the intellect gets destroyed; and when the intellect is destroyed, one is ruined.'

Pay heed to the statement by Mark Twain: 'Anger is an acid that can do more harm to the vessel in which it is stored than to anything on which it is poured.'

Realizing the devastating effects of rage, resolve firmly to not be a slave to it. Here are some techniques to help you tame anger.

Recognize your anger. Awareness of your weakness will help 'catch it' before the spark turns into a blaze. When we are angry, we clench our hands or jaws, breathe faster or pace up and down. Also, our shoulders grow tense, and we develop knots in our stomach. Learn to recognize these cues and pacify your anger at this stage itself. A consistent and disciplined yoga and meditation practice will help grow your awareness slowly.

Identify your triggers. Detect people, situations or activities that trigger feelings of anger. Maybe you get upset when people are not aligned to your way of doing things or do not share your values. Or when your spouse is not willing to compromise and imposes his/her desires on you. Or when your child does not follow your instructions.

Become aware of the triggers and neutralize them by changing your interpretation of them. Work on your internal talk by reframing your perspective. Will this matter in six months or six years from now? Be open to any outcome—let go of 'should' and 'must'. Do not make assumptions; do not blame others; take responsibility for your thoughts and actions; and share your feelings with the other person without getting emotional.

Delay and control your angry response. Once you identify the start of the angry state, you must break the reflex response cycle. Your right brain is the source of your emotions, while the left brain is the one that reasons and analyses the benefits and harms.

In the heat of the moment, the initial retaliatory response is from the right side of the brain. It is neither logical nor rational. But within a gap of a few minutes, the left brain produces another response. This is more logical and reasonable. Hence, if you delay your response when angry, you are likely to respond appropriately and constructively.

Choose from some of the recommended actions below for delaying your response as well as subduing your anger.

- Inhale for four seconds, hold your breath for four seconds and exhale for four seconds. Keep breathing deeply for a few minutes until you feel calmer.
- Count from 1 to 60 to allow a minute to balance your emotions.
- Chant the Names of God or visualize His form.
- Take a quick walk down your office hallway or up the stairs or perform yoga.

Anticipate the conflict. Parents prone to anger know ahead of time that if their child brings home a poor report card, they will be angry and will most certainly lose their cool. To prevent getting angry, prepare the responses in advance. You can rehearse your concerns and practise what you feel is the best way to handle the situation.

Sublimate your desires towards the Divine. Anger is a symptom of a greater disease within our psyche—desire. Let us briefly deconstruct desire.

When our mind gets attached, it leads to desire. If the positive or negative desire is fulfilled, all remains well. But if our desire gets thwarted, we become annoyed. So, how can we overcome this? The Bhagavad Gita presents the solution:

viṣhayā vinivartante nirāhārasya dehinaḥ
rasa-varjaṁ raso 'pyasya paraṁ dṛiṣhṭvā nivartate   (2.59)

'Aspirants may restrain the senses from their objects of enjoyment, but the taste for the sense objects remains. However, even this taste ceases for those who realize the Supreme.'

So, replace your material desires with divine yearnings—the desire to serve, the desire to glorify the Lord, the desire for divine knowledge, and so on. Spiritual aspirations elevate and purify the mind because the object of attachment is pure. Purity of mind naturally eradicates anger from the root.

44

Forgiveness: Let Go of Resentment

Yes, we have all been wronged and betrayed, hurt and harmed. Perhaps a co-worker sabotaged a project. Your partner turned out to be a cheater. You grew up in a traumatic environment or were abused. We have gone through negative experiences that may have left their mark on our psyche. And even years later, we find ourselves seething with anger and resentment.

Emotional hurts are difficult to deal with because, unlike physical injuries, the wound is deep within. Thus, they can easily leave us shattered and disoriented. We justify grudges based on our physical and mental anguish. The uneasiness makes us feel that something needs to change. That change comes through the practise of forgiveness.

Forgiveness is a gift we bestow upon ourselves. Nothing helps overcome emotional hurt more effectively than pardoning the offender. The conscious decision to release vengeful emotions sets your mind free. The other may not necessarily deserve it, but the mental release restores your peace of mind and brings closure to the matter.

Having said that, practising forgiveness is not always easy. One of the best ways to inspire yourself to forgive is to remind yourself of its various benefits, and also remember the drawbacks of ignoring it.

The benefits of forgiveness are manifold. Practising forgiveness has been associated with hopefulness and happiness. A reduction in anger is also observed in people who forgive. The act has further been linked to lower blood pressure and improved cardiovascular health.

In addition, forgiveness offers many other material and spiritual rewards. It repairs and heals broken relationships because it begins with empathy for the one who hurt you. And even if you part ways with the one who wronged you, forgiving helps you move on in life with compassion and acceptance. It frees you from the victim mentality in which external factors are blamed and puts you in control of your emotions.

Lack of forgiveness comes at a tremendous price. When we resent somebody's behaviour, the negativity acts like poison on our heart. Someone put it beautifully, 'Harbouring bitterness is like drinking poison in the hope that it will kill the other.'

Consequently, feelings of bitterness and injustice cause even more harm than the wrongful act itself. This is the reason why all great spiritual teachers and religious traditions around the world emphasize practising forgiveness.

Choosing to forgive is a choice you make for your own peace, not for the other. Having understood its value, let us discuss some effective mindsets and techniques to implement it.

Shift the way you look at the past. Let go of bygones. You do not have to hold onto grievances for the rest of your life. You cannot change the past. So, do not keep reliving it in your mind. Realize that the situation has passed. It is your own thoughts that are preventing you from embracing new beginnings that await you.

Do not talk critically about those who hurt you. Talking about wrongful actions and persons can solidify the memory in your mind. And in a subtle way, it gives you an excuse to not forgive. Speaking ill of others reignites the emotional pain and increases the sense of entitlement. Refrain from rehashing the past not just to yourself but to others as well. This will loosen your negative attachment to the person who cheated you or to the incident that harmed you.

Develop empathy. Try seeing the situation from the other person's point of view, which may shed light on why they acted the way they did. Also, remember that people can only behave to the level of their emotional maturity. See them through the lens of empathy.

Recollect the times you made the mistake of hurting others. You will then find it easier to discover compassion in your heart for those who behave ill with you. Remember, 'To err is human, to forgive, divine.'

The lives of saintly people are replete with inspiring stories of how they forgave their wrongdoers, and even succeeded in winning them over with their love and benevolence. Here is a telling story from Mahatma Gandhi's life.

While he was living in South Africa, a person made an attempt on his life. Gandhiji refused to hate the man. He said, 'I shall love him and win his love.'

One year later, that same man came to apologize before Gandhiji and wept for forgiveness.

This is the characteristic of great personalities—they refuse to allow their minds to dwell on hatred for anyone.

Adopt the spiritual perspective. Learn and grow from your suffering. You can even find spiritual meaning in your suffering. For example, emotional hurt can serve as an eye-opener about the real nature of worldly relatives. Or perhaps, it can make you realize that God alone is your true Companion. In this way, you can see each pain as a blessing in disguise.

Forgiveness is a sublime personality trait and a sign of spiritual evolvement. It is critical to your self-purification. It may not be easy, but it is necessary. With practise, it will become second nature to you. That will be the day you will have arrived spiritually.

45

Keys to a Happy Married Life

'Marriages are made in heaven,' is a common saying. However, to make married life successful, no heavenly help will arrive. The two partners must work together towards building and strengthening their wedlock. Every marriage is different because there are thousands of variables. However, some basic rules can help couples lead a fulfilling married life.

Respect and honour your partner's independence. Though marriage is a union of two individuals, it is important for both to also be independently happy. A joyful person spreads happiness everywhere.

It is natural for each person to have different likes and dislikes based on their unique experiences, upbringing and *sanskārs*. Therefore, in a marriage, independence and personal space are important for both individuals to grow.

For example, the husband likes cricket while the wife likes to listen to Indian classical music. So, the husband must occasionally accompany his wife to a classical music concert. Similarly, sometimes, the wife can watch a cricket match with her husband. At the very least, she can happily allow her husband to enjoy the match with his friends.

Having said that, you must ensure that in the name of autonomy, you do not compromise with your partner on important values and goals.

Discuss. It can sort out things that war cannot. That is the power of verbal interaction. In a marriage, there should be regular dialogue between the two partners. Every important decision—be it family, finances or friends—should involve sufficient discussion and exchange of ideas.

Reading the newspaper when your wife wants to have a conversation with you or raising the volume of the television when your husband wants to say something, are not good ways of communicating. Sometimes, the other does not say anything in words but communicates with body language. Hence, be attentive.

Avoid getting into arguments. If either the wife or the husband gets angry, the other person should avoid an argument and back down. The matter can be taken up for discussion again when the atmosphere is neutral. **Getting into an argument leads to a clash of egos, which only increases the distance between individuals.** Do read more on communication in the chapter, 'Communicate Effectively'.

Share responsibilities. Life is easier when responsibilities are shared between the couple. It can be household chores, taking care of children, handling finances or other duties. When each knows and acknowledges the other's effort, it becomes easier. It is not necessary that each responsibility be divided equally. Instead, the goal should be that that no one feels overburdened.

Raising children can also be a major point of contention as both have different experiences and viewpoints. To avoid conflict, it is better to discuss responsibilities regarding children and how to raise them.

Be grateful and expressive. Many times, people take the effort made by the other half for granted. When it goes unnoticed, frustration creeps in. Gradually, it leads to resentment and anger and then to a crack in the relationship. Sometimes, the partner may be appreciative but does not say it out loud. It is always better to be expressive. Words of encouragement can inspire the other person to work harder.

Be supportive when the going gets tough. While one should be supportive at all times, the partner should put in extra effort, especially when the chips are down. Difficulties can come in many forms—loss of a job, financial shortfall, death of a close relative, and so forth.

During such times, people need additional assurance. Tough times wreck self-assurance. People become irritated and sentimental. At this time, the last thing one wishes to hear is 'I told you so'. It is during these times that the partner can step up, boost confidence and support like a rock.

You may ask, 'Swamiji, you are a renounced sanyasi. What qualification do you have to explain this topic?' Well, not direct experience, but I have lots of indirect experience. During my travels as a monk, I have lived with over a thousand families and witnessed their travails, besides counselling many more. I do hope the advice in this chapter will help you avoid the mess I have seen in so many homes.

46

Effective Ways to Raise Children

A new-born child brings immense joy to parents but also augments responsibilities. As they grow, their requirements change, and most parents work hard to fulfil them. All parents want nothing but the best for their children.

However, giving children the latest toy, sending them to the best school, enrolling for tuition classes, and the like might not be enough. Here are a few pointers to raise successful children.

Raising children is both an art and a science. Every child is different and so are its needs. One size does not fit all. Also, young children must be dealt with differently than teenagers. The ancient books of wisdom advise:

> *lālyet pancha varṣhāṇī daśha varṣhāṇī tādyet*
>
> (*Chanakya Neeti*)

'For the first five years, shower love upon your child to facilitate the blossoming of their personality. Then for the next 10 years, along with offering love, discipline your child with strictness.'

This chapter has sections on both. But let us first start with some general principles that apply to children of all ages.

Be happy and lead by example. Children who live in happy families do well compared to children who live in high-conflict families. If the parents fight or are not polite to each other, then that is what the child learns. If either of the parents is depressed, the child is more likely to have behavioural problems. Therefore, it is important to create a happy atmosphere at home.

Talk and listen to children. Parents should take out a few minutes daily to have a conversation with their children. With complete and undivided attention. The time spent talking while watching TV or scrolling through the mobile phone does not count as quality time.

Back-and-forth exchanges with children even as young as 3–5 years and involving them in the decision-making process at home helps them develop communication skills and increases their overall satisfaction in life.

Encourage them to set high goals. If you tell your child something with conviction, they will believe it and work towards it. Encourage children to set high goals and work hard for them. Help them realize the immense potential that God has bestowed in them.

Praise efforts, not results. Some parents and teachers only focus on results. This reduces the ability of the child to accept failure. It is better to encourage the effort and motivate children to give their best, without being fixated on results. Such an attitude enables children to face failures as adults without getting stressed. After all, **failure is a stepping stone to success**, so why be scared of it?

Involve them in home chores, such as helping set up the dinner table, cleaning their room and watering the plants. Children who help with chores at home will grow up more sociable and have better relationships with other children. This lays the groundwork to becoming good team members in future.

After these general set of guidelines for all age groups, let us turn our focus to young children between the ages of 1–12 years.

Limit screen time; instead, read to them daily. First televisions and now mobile phones have made reading books to children an old-fashioned habit. Parents find it easy to give an iPad or tablet to appease their children and keep them occupied.

On the other hand, reading books to kids improves bonding, increases their attention span and instils a habit of lifelong learning. So, dust off that children's book and start reading to your child from today.

More playtime for the kids. Today, even tiny tots are being burdened under a huge load of academics. That robs children of playtime. But scientists say that unstructured time or games period in school brings about positive changes in the brain. Playing develops the neuron connections in the front part of the brain. This helps in creativity, problem-solving and several other functions needed for the child's happiness.

As children grow and enter the teenage years, they go through a lot of changes both physically and mentally; they also push their boundaries emotionally to see how far they can go. Keeping this in mind, parents should use a different approach for teenagers. Let us look at a few important points here.

Observe and listen attentively. Rebellious nature, impulsive decisions, tantrums and argumentativeness are usually seen during the teenage years. Being too strict or being too lenient, both can be counterproductive.

As a parent, it is essential to be a good listener, without sounding nosy, as that would help break the ice and win the confidence of your teenage child. Even if the teenager hurts your sentiments, as an adult yourself, keep your patience and try your best to refrain from reacting negatively.

Further, any major change in mood, behaviour or habits of your teen is a warning sign that should be investigated. Do not be judgemental of their mistakes. Show your support to reassure them that you are there for them, no matter what.

Strengthen the bond. Engage in mutually enjoyable activities such as watching movies, music shows and sports events. This will strengthen your bond, and the chances are that the teen will gradually open up. Eating dinner together is also a good way to connect.

Be firm when needed and watch their friend circle. During the teenage years, children are very vulnerable to bad habits like smoking and drinking. These can wreak havoc on the teen's young mind. If you sense that your teenager is going astray, you need to immediately put your foot down, and if required, set curfews and clear rules regarding your disapproval for such things.

Although during teenage years, friends take priority over parents, do not worry. Know and meet the friends of your teens to find out who they spend time with. If you find that the company is bad, talk to your child and explain the consequences. If needed, be firm and gradually restrain your child from spending time with the wrong friends.

Career choice. Parents should identify their child's talents early and nudge them in the right direction. Every child is different. Even though regular studies are important, your child's interest may not necessarily be academics. It could be fine arts, sports, entrepreneurship or something else. Proper nurturing of their interests and talents under a qualified teacher or institute will prove helpful.

Some parents want to get their career desires fulfilled through their children. If the parent could not become a doctor, they want their child to become one. That only leads to frustration and burdens the child with a profession they may despise. Hence, as a responsible parent, you should resist this temptation of imposing your desires on your child.

Along with the above-mentioned steps, raising a child with good values and character is of utmost importance.

47

Establish Boundaries in Relationships

Boundaries are our personal comfort levels beyond which we do not allow anyone to push us. Life requires us to balance our individual needs alongside our responsibilities to others. Setting boundaries helps us do that. They are required in both professional and personal dealings.

People will ride rough shod over you if you have not proper set boundaries. They will expect access to you 24/7. They will make it your responsibility to keep them happy. They will make you feel guilty for not fulfilling their request. Without boundaries, people will intrude your privacy and deplete your energies.

If someone repeatedly refuses to take 'No' for an answer, he is violating your boundaries. If you explained to someone that you cannot take her calls, and yet she keeps at it, she is transgressing your limits.

Do you know your rights? You have the right to say 'No' when asked for a favour. You have the right to spend time on yourself. You have the right to decide what is important to you and what is not. You have the right to decide the level of privacy you need.

What do healthy boundaries look like? A healthy boundary is when a teacher, on the first day of class, tells her students the rules of conduct. When a new mother asks her husband to focus on his responsibility with their baby, so that she can have some time for herself. When working professionals refuse to connect with their clients on social media.

What do unhealthy boundaries look like? The sign that you have not set good boundaries is when you agree to your manager's request, 'Could you finish up my work for me? I have a company dinner.' When your spouse says, 'I get jealous when you go out with your friends. So, stay home with me.' When you stop going for satsang, since it makes your siblings unhappy, and so forth.

WOULD YOU SLOW DOWN YOUR BREATHING? NOW YOU'VE STARTED USING THE OXYGEN MEANT FOR ME!

If you can identify with any of the above situations, you direly need to learn the art of setting boundaries.

Communicate openly and honestly. Healthy boundaries are established and sustained by openly expressing them. It is important to let others know what you are comfortable with and what makes you uneasy. This may be required for financial, emotional and physical matters.

For example, in some cultures, people are very friendly and embrace one another when meeting. In other cultures, they prefer to greet each other without touching. Similarly, some people need privacy, while others do not. If you do not clearly communicate your preferences and needs, people can make assumptions and cross your comfort level. Hence, to avoid misunderstandings, communicate your limits and expectations to others.

Learn to say 'No'. We all have fixed resources of time, energy and effort. How we utilize them determines our efficacy in achieving our goals. When we prioritize our list of to-dos, we put the most important and urgent tasks up top, while things requiring least attention go to the bottom of the list. In this manner, we say 'Yes' to some and 'No' to others.

Apply the same principle to your relationships. While you should be helpful and available to do the needful for others, you must learn to say 'No' to demands that are unimportant or wasteful. After all, you also have a responsibility towards your own goals. For that, you must avoid people who drain your energy or overtake your space. Warren Buffett put it nicely: 'The difference between successful people and really successful people is that really successful people say no to almost everything.'

Do not let others take advantage of you. You may have heard the proverb: 'Give them an inch and they'll take a mile.' If you make a concession, people sometimes misconstrue it as a weakness and take as much as they can, leaving you high and dry.

Let us say, you were kind enough to lend an item to your neighbour in need. But now, he has made it a habit of asking you for help daily, instead of securing other means to fulfil his needs. By the same token, children who are not reprimanded are found taking advantage of their parents' leniency.

Here is the two-step solution for it.

1. Take responsibility for your lack of control over the situation. You did not let the other know how far they are permitted to go.

2. Hold others accountable with firm consequences for crossing boundaries. That may mean not speaking to someone for a certain period of time, not being readily available, not responding to social media messages or even going to the extent of reprimanding, if necessary.

The intention here is not to punish, rather to clarify a mutually respectful relationship. Thus, it should be done with empathy in the heart, not with a feeling of revenge.

Unworkable situations. Abusive or violent circumstances are often beyond the stage of reform. They have crossed all limits and taken on an agonizing shape. Such situations can call for stern and courageous action. If faced with verbal, emotional or physical abuse, it is best to confide in a trusted source and take appropriate steps to remove yourself from it. This can include walking away from the situation for your protection.

Drop all boundaries with God. While we maintain boundaries in the world, we should become free of them in the Divine realm. Why? We set limits to protect ourselves in the world, but God is our Supreme Shelter. God is compassionate and has the purest of intentions for all souls. Though the world may cheat us, He is perfectly just and fair. His wishes, expressed in the sacred texts, can be adhered to and followed without any doubts.

Hence, always harbour the 'Yes' attitude with your Supreme Lord by following the teachings of the scriptures and your Guru. **By dropping pretences and being humble in front of God and Guru, we become the recipient of Their infinite grace and blessings.**

48

Grieving for a Loved One

One of the most painful experiences in life is the loss of a loved one. Our natural response to it is grief. This is the emotional torment we experience when someone we dearly love is taken away from us. Since the death of a near one is such a significant loss, the grief it triggers is also very intense. In fact, for parents, the death of a child can be the single biggest stressor in life.

Unfortunately, most people face a situation of bereavement sometime or the other in their life. It could be the death of parents, a lifelong partner, close friends or relatives. Often, the emotional suffering it causes can become extremely overwhelming, leading to disruption of health, and even absence of sleep. Bouncing back from such setbacks poses an immense challenge. But, as we shall see in this chapter, if it is handled well, it can lead to substantial growth of the soul.

Prepare for shock and disbelief. Immediately after a loved one dies, you may have trouble believing it really happened. You could even keep expecting them to show up. This is more common when someone dies suddenly. Because of disbelief, you may be unable to cry and show much emotion. Instead, if you have been preparing for a loved one's death for a long time, you would usually not experience denial or disbelief.

If you are in this stage, resist the urge to shut down, go numb or pretend that the loved one has not died. Such suppression will backfire—the emotions could then manifest in the physical body as fatigue, muscle aches, allergies, hypertension and even cardiac arrest. Unresolved grief can even lead to complications, such as substance abuse or depression.

Accept bereavement as a normal human reaction and decide to work through the pain to heal yourself. You will have to tend to the emotional wound and cure it, just as you do with physical wounds.

It may help to know that there are five stages of grief: denial, anger, guilt, sadness and acceptance. However, there is no neat and sequential order to them, because everyone's grief is as individual as their lives. We have discussed the first stage— denial. Now let us see the others.

Expect to feel anger. Once the reality of the loved one's death dawns, you may feel resentful. You could blame God for what you perceive as injustice. You may hold the doctors responsible for not having saved the person or for not having done their job well. Or you could even feel let down by the person for abandoning you.

Counter these sentiments by reminding yourself that they will not help in any way. They will not bring back the departed person. Instead, adopt a proactive stance—the departure of your loved one has created a problem in your life, and you need to focus on the solution rather than simply repeating the problem in your mind over and over again.

Expect to feel guilt. In this stage, people somehow feel responsible for what has happened. They blame themselves for not doing enough to prevent the death, even if there was nothing more they could have done. They could even feel guilty about their own feelings—relief or lack of emotions—when the person dies after a long and terrible illness.

If you find yourself thinking, 'If only I had done this thing differently', you are probably in this stage of grief. Remember that these are common human emotions, but almost always, baseless. Further, your loved one's death was not God's way of punishing you. Everyone comes and goes by their own karmic account.

Expect to feel sad. This is the most universal symptom of bereavement. In this stage, your thoughts may oscillate between despair, emptiness and loneliness. They may even exacerbate to depression. 'I am too sad to do anything', 'I do not find interest in anything', 'What's the purpose of living?', and the like.

Resist the urge to drown your intellect in alcohol or drugs. They may relieve you for a few hours but will make your recovery more difficult in the long run. And you could even come under the grip of substance abuse as a lifelong vice. So, beware of the lure of intoxicants.

After a loved one's death, people often have difficulty in eating, sleeping and exercising. For that reason, they tend to ignore these self-maintenance activities. But bear in mind that grieving can quickly deplete your vital energy. As the mind and body are connected, grieving makes you susceptible to stress, fatigue, and a plethora of physical and mental afflictions.

Therefore, in this phase of your life, it is more important than ever to take care of yourself. Exercise regularly. It will elevate your mood and serve as a welcome distraction. Also, ensure that you take regular nutritious meals. If you feel energized, you will cope better with the emotional turmoil too.

Accept the loss and move on. All cultures and traditions prescribe periods of mourning. These rituals provide an opportunity to come to terms with the changed situation, and then to stop looking back and move on in life. In the Hindu tradition, there is usually a 13-day period of bereavement and rituals. The practice is supposedly for the benefit of the departed soul, but factually, it provides the family members a mechanism to accept the altered circumstances and cope with the loss. The expectation is that by the end of the mourning period, everyone will be sufficiently healed to return to regular work.

Spiritual wisdom makes acceptance of loss so much easier. Let us now see how this happens.

Spiritual journey through bereavement. The Vedic texts inform us that the soul is immortal—it is neither born nor does it die. Just as we change old clothes to put on new ones, what we think of as death is simply the soul changing bodies. By repeatedly contemplating on this knowledge, we can dispel our emotional suffering. For instance, when Bali, the monkey king, died, and his wife Tara was lamenting, Lord Ram explained to her:

pragaṭa so tanu tava āgeṅ sovā,

  jīva nitya kehi lagi tumha rovā   (Ramayan)

'If you are grieving for your husband's body, it is lying before you. If you are grieving for his soul, it is eternal. Then why lament?' Therefore, the most powerful ladder for climbing out of the vortex of emotional suffering is divine knowledge.

Further, the sacred books teach us to change our perspective towards tragedies. By altering the way we look at reversals, we can transform the reality of our life. The celestial sage, Narad, states:

  lokahānau chintā na kāryā niveditātmalokavedatvāt

  (*Narad Bhakti Darshan,* sutra 61)

'If you experience a reversal in the world, do not become anxious; rather, see it as a form of God's grace.' Sage Narad suggests that we see the loss as an opportunity to free our mind from material associations. Consequently, the so-called adversity turns to our advantage.

Daily contemplation on these principles will slowly help develop the strength to rise above grief and similar emotions. And then, the day will finally come when we will realize the import of Lord Krishna's words:

  gatāsūn-agatāsūnśh-cha nānuśhochanti paṇḍitāḥ

  (Bhagavad Gita verse 2.11)

'Those who are wise grieve neither for the living nor for the dead.'

Section Four

....

PROFESSIONAL FULFILMENT

49

Choose Your Profession Carefully

Most people spend almost one-third of their time on their job. Which means, you will spend about 80,000 hours on your profession over a 40-year career, estimating you work 50 weeks a year and 40 hours a week. And this is a conservative figure considering the long hours most people put in.

If you dislike the work you do, then a major portion of your daily routine will be a drab or even a torture. Instead, if you choose a profession that you find meaningful and enjoyable, then without any ado, one-third of your day will be immensely blissful and soulfully satisfying. We will discuss here how to find a career that is best for you.

Money—how important is it? Undoubtedly, it is necessary for procuring comforts and luxuries that will ensure the standard of living you desire. Yet, money cannot improve your emotional well-being. To decide on your dream job, here are some other factors you must look at.

The nature of work must be engaging. Job satisfaction comes not from the salary you earn but from what you do hour-by-hour and day-by-day. If you find the work absorbing, then it holds your attention and helps you get into a state of flow.

There must be ample opportunities to learn and grow. The biggest reason for boredom at work is flattening of the learning curve. When people feel that their work is monotonous and tedious, they become uninterested. Job satisfaction is high when opportunities to learn and master new skills keep coming.

The work should be challenging. When asked what kind of job they would like, most people say, 'One that is not too stressful.'

However, experience shows that undemanding work is undesirable because it becomes dull and uninteresting. Fulfilment comes from work that challenges you. But if the challenge is beyond your perceived abilities, it becomes too stressful. Therefore, a suitable job for you would be one that pushes you beyond your comfort zone but not so far that you suffer mental anguish.

The work should make a difference to society. This is one of the key ingredients to life satisfaction. Our work gives us an avenue to give back to the community in multiple ways. When we perceive that it is benefitting others, it causes great satisfaction. We feel that our efforts are of good use.

Choose work that you are good at. When you do something well, the sense of achievement is a huge source of happiness. Further, your expertise and abilities give you greater power to negotiate the best jobs and remunerations in your field. You get to work on important projects.

A supportive work environment is a big plus. According to the *Harvard Business Review*, most people quit their jobs because they do not like their boss.[17] Conversely, 'social support' is one of the biggest predictors of job satisfaction. Since relationships are so important, the opportunity for supportive friendships at work makes a big difference.

People who succeed in their profession are the ones who find fulfilment, meaning and growth opportunities in their work. Therefore, choose your career and your job thoughtfully. Remember, you will be spending almost one-third of your adult life at work.

---

[17]'Why People Quit Their Jobs', *Harvard Business Review*, September 2016, https://bit.ly/3ADWZ0S. Accessed on 14 June 2022.

50

Make Your Work into Play

'Do what you love, and you will never have to work another day in your life.' This advice is immensely popular and appears so attractive. It is a favourite line of motivational speakers and personality development coaches. Hearing it, people think they need to switch to a career that they are insanely passionate about. They must find a profession that will make their whole life feel like one huge vacation on a cruise.

But is this advice correct? Let's find out.

Your biggest passion is not always a realistic career path. How many little boys in India want to be Test cricketers, and how many in the US dream to be NBA basketball players? How many little girls wish to be singers and musicians? Yet, only one amongst millions who aspire, becomes talented enough to make these passions into successful careers. The rest must remember that play does not pay the bills for the standard of living you want. You must work for it.

As I travel the world, I come across hundreds of musicians, wellness practitioners, painters, yoga teachers and writers who are struggling to make ends meet. So, before jumping into your passion as your career, analyse if it can provide for your lifelong needs.

Trying to follow your passion can needlessly limit your career options. For example, if you are passionate about art, it is easy to think you must become an artist to have a satisfying career. But people do not remain passionate about the same thing all through their lives. As they grow emotionally and spiritually, their interests also change.

So, overemphasizing passion during youth could make you neglect other factors that are immensely important in determining job satisfaction. Read about them in the previous chapter 'Choose Your Profession Carefully'.

Play can have two connotations. If it means to work on something that is deeply interesting to us, that is great. But if the notion is that work should be all fun and entertainment, its effects can be disastrous. The *Kathopanishad* explains the consequences of unwholesome 'fun':

> *tayoḥ śhreya ādadānasya sādhu*
> *bhavati hīyate 'rthādya u preyo vṛiṇīte*   (1.2.1)

'There are two kinds of pleasure—*preya and śhreya. Preya* is enjoyment that is immensely sweet at first but later turns into poison. The reverse is *śhreya*—bliss that initially seems like poison but later becomes like nectar.'

Western scholars talk about *hedonia* and *eudaemonia*. Hedonic fun—named after Hedon, the Greek god of pleasure—is short-lived enjoyment. The other, eudaemonia, is lasting satisfaction that comes from accomplishment. Eudaemonic happiness requires laborious toil, but it creates excellence and lasting benefit.

No doubt, entertainment is thrilling, but it is a lower kind of thrill that does not last. We enjoy it for a few hours and then it is gone. **The higher kind of fulfilment that satisfies our soul—and remains day and night—comes from meaningful work. This requires sacrifice and austerities.** So, do try to incorporate fun into your workplace, but do not expect your entire career to be a cocktail party with friends.

Then what does it mean to 'make your work into play'? It means doing productive work, which you find so interesting that even its austerities seem like great fun.

The highest satisfaction comes from knowing that our work is making a difference to the world—in small or big ways—and in doing it, we are using all our talents to the best of our ability.

Every job will undoubtedly have its irksome aspects. Just as you cannot get a 'perfect' life partner, you cannot also get a 'perfect' job. There are always traits of your spouse that you must tolerate. Similarly, professional positions come with their share of pesky chores and tiresome responsibilities. These are not the most enjoyable, but you must bear with them if you want a meaningful career path.

'Do what you love, and you will never work another day in your life' is a well-meaning sentiment. But remember, it should satisfy two important points. First, your work must provide the practical necessity of the standard of living you want in life. Second, it must not be construed as absence of toil and hardship. Rather, it should be work that you feel is fulfilling as per your value system.

51

How to Make Your Hobby Your Career

Are you dissatisfied with your profession? Do you feel that your passion lies elsewhere, and you are stuck doing what does not interest you? If it is any solace, do know that you are not alone. Over 80 per cent of corporate professionals around the world are unhappy with their work.[18]

Did you get into a wrong career? The reasons for making a wrong career choice could be numerous. Possibly, when you started in your profession, you were not sufficiently aware of what it would entail. Maybe, you got pushed into a vocation, against your choice, by parents and relatives.

It could also be that you discovered a cause outside your occupation that holds great meaning for you. So, you wish to move to it. Whatever be the reason for your present career seeming ill-suited, what should you do now? Should you simply carry on with the job that you dislike, or should you venture to switch to one more aligned with your passion?

When to change your path? Here is some practical advice.

---

[18]'80% of corporate professionals unhappy with current performance management system: Survey', *The Hindu BusinessLine*, 20 October 2020, https://bit.ly/3MJOlAQ. Accessed on 14 June 2022.

If you continue the profession you dislike, you could end up spending around 80,000 hours of your life in sheer misery. That cannot be anybody's idea of a good life. Hence, it is undoubtedly worth your while to explore a career switch. This may entail going back to college full-time for a new course of study or taking part-time classes to eventually make the change.

Hobby as career? As we discussed in the previous chapter, it would be great if our life's passion and hobby could become a good source of income. But there is no guarantee that following your passion will bring the bread on the table. If you have the responsibility of providing for your children and spouse, you cannot afford to take risks. Besides, it may be too late in life to start a new career all over again.

The practical and realistic option. Do not quit your present work—it is after all meeting your physical needs and providing you financial security. Instead, do it in a spirit of karm yog. This will provide you the strength to tolerate the ugly aspects of your job.

Yet, do not neglect your passion either—it will give meaning and purpose to your life. Hence, pursue it on the side as a hobby. Make time for it in the evenings or work on it during the weekends. It will enrich the quality of your life and make it purposeful.

And it is possible that if your hobby grows sufficiently, the day may come when you can replace your present career with it. But until then, practise your hobby on the side.

52

Cultivate a Growth Mindset

There are always a few exceptional people who dazzle us with their excellence. We observe this in all fields, whether it is their business acumen, leadership qualities or technical wizardry. Some people are just too good at what they do. When you see these phenomenally successful people, what is the thought that comes to your mind?

Do you tell yourself, 'They were born with special talents. They won the DNA lottery.'

Or do you think to yourself, 'Wow! Imagine how hard they would have practised. If I hope to emulate them, I must also work hard.'

Did you pick the first answer or the second? And I hope you did not skip the exercise, because it will reveal something especially important about your nature.

Fixed mindset. If you chose the first answer, you have a fixed mindset based on which you think: 'Some have it, some don't.' People with this attitude believe that their abilities are fixed or predetermined by birth. So, they do not work to improve their competencies. When they face setbacks, they get caught up in self-pity and hopelessness. Consequently, they remain stuck in mediocrity throughout life.

People with a fixed mindset say things like 'I can never get that promotion, I am not smart enough', or 'I'm too old to learn new skills now' or 'This is how I've always been; I can't change now'.

Growth mindset. If you chose the second answer, you possess a growth mindset. People with this attitude believe that people's knowledge and skills can be developed through effort. They do not claim that everyone can become a Ramanujam, but they do believe everyone can become far better through effort and practise.

Consequently, when faced with a setback, the growth mindset people reframe it as a learning opportunity. Instead of giving up, they put in extra effort to become even better, and thereby ensure success.

A scientific research finding you must know. *Carol Dweck, a psychologist from Stanford, researched these two mindsets for several decades.*[19] *She would offer psychological tests to students for determining whether they had a fixed mindset or growth mindset.*

Then she would ask them to choose between easy and difficult problems. Those with a fixed mindset invariably chose the easy one—their highest priority was to ensure they did not fail. While those with the growth mindset selected the difficult problem—they saw it as an opportunity to challenge themselves and grow. Dweck observed that this second category cared more about learning than

[19]Dweck, Carol S., 'The Secret to Raising Smart Kids', Scientific American, 1 January 2015, https://bit.ly/3zMEHu1. Accessed on 25 June 2022.

getting good grades. They were eager to know their deficiencies and improve, not hide them.

When it came to performance, the students with a growth mindset were predicted to have greater academic success compared to their cohorts in the study.

The same contrasting attitudes are carried forward in the professional realm. Those believing that success is only for the 'gifted' prefer easy jobs. They avoid challenges because they are too scared to fail. In contrast, those with a growth mentality love to be tested. They learn better, perform better and deal better with impediments.

'I was born that way' is the enemy of progress. If you want to grow and accomplish more in your career, then focus on constant learning. Remember the Law of Infinite Potential:

> All souls have infinite potential for growth, whatever be their present state.
>
> —Swami Mukundananda in
> *7 Divine Laws to Awaken Your Best Self*

In this law, the word 'potential' is most important. It will kindle optimism for the future and encourage you to aim high.

But what should one do if they realize they have been harbouring the wrong mindset all their life? Do not be discouraged. It takes time and effort to change your thinking, but it can definitely be done. Here are some steps that can help.

Become aware of your fixed mindset. Take some time to introspect and become aware of your defective thinking. A faulty mindset results from flawed beliefs about yourself and the world. So, work on changing your beliefs regarding abilities and success. You can read about the process in the chapter, 'Choose Your Beliefs Well'.

Respond with a 'growth mindset'. Let us say you have landed a new sales job but are unable to meet your quota. The choice you have is: what to think in this situation? Either you can decide you are incapable, or you can say to yourself, 'I am not a good salesperson, but I will work hard to learn the art.'

Keep in mind that you can choose what to think at every moment. You can either frame a setback as 'the end of the world' or as 'an opportunity to keep growing'.

J.K. Rowling, author of Harry Potter, *was rejected 12 times before her book was accepted for publishing. If she had given up after the first rejection, the* Harry Potter *series would not have been the success it is today, with 500 million in worldwide sales.*

Get out of your safe haven. The choice to respond with a growth mindset requires leaving the safety of your comfort zone, which is never easy. So, remember the saying: 'Comfort zone is a beautiful thing, but nothing ever grows there.'

If you do not stretch yourself and experience discomfort, you will never grow in any area of your life. Are you nervous about giving a presentation, give it anyway! Are you tired of chasing customers, chase them anyway! Slowly you will start to expand your level of comfort, and that is the only way to grow.

53

Commit to Excellence in Everything You Do

*O*nce a devotee visited a temple, where a sculptor was working *on an idol. He noticed an identical statue nearby and asked, 'Do you need two identical idols?'*

Without looking up, the sculptor responded, 'No, I need only one. The other one is damaged.'

The gentleman examined the two statues closely but could see no apparent damage. The sculptor pointed to the scratch on the nose of the discarded idol. On learning that the statue was to be placed 20 feet high, the gentleman was perplexed and commented, 'But who would even know of the scratch from that far?'

The sculptor smiled and quietly stated, 'I know it, and God knows it.'

The mindset of excellence is a way of thinking where you give your best to whatever you do. People with this attitude do not believe in taking the easy lackadaisical route. Instead, they live by the philosophy: 'If anything is worth doing at all, it is worth doing well.'

Such people approach even small tasks with sincerity and

dedication. They exert themselves. They think deeply and pay attention to detail, and consequently manifest tremendous quality in their works. It is this mindset that produces exceptional scientists, athletes, musicians and industrialists.

Why is excellence important? You could as well ask, 'Why is the moon important when there are a million stars in the sky?' The answer is: Because all by itself, the moon outshines all the stars put together. Likewise, excellence makes a huge difference. One phenomenal innovator contributes more to the world than myriads of 'also-rans'.

The legendary Steve Jobs gave the world many innovations that changed the way we live. He expressed his commitment to excellence in these words: 'We do not get a chance to do that many things, and everyone should be really excellent. Because this is our life.'

The culture he imparted to Apple continues after him. Even today, the company's products are renowned for their quality and reliability.

The same applies to all areas of life.

Ramakrishna Paramahansa had hundreds of disciples, among whom Swami Vivekananda was one. But his impact on the world was more than that of all his guru-bhais put together. That was because he went the extra mile and toiled the extra sweat. He made his Guru's instruction his life and soul. He contemplated deeply on how to fulfil it. He prepared himself through arduous sadhana. And he dared to venture into unchartered terrain. He was the moon among his spiritual brothers, who made his

Guru famous around the world.

Excellence pleases God. The talents and skills we were born with are God's gift to us. How we develop and use them will be our gift to Him. If, by being lazy, we squander away our potential, it disrespects the One who entrusted us with it. The Bible states: 'To whom much is given, from him much is expected.' (Luke 12.48)

Why excellence is so rare. Because it is difficult, while mediocrity is easy. Excellence requires practising many divine virtues: the dedication to push yourself to your max, even though it pains. The willingness to remain focused, even when distractions are easily available. The thirst to seek that one gem of knowledge which could make all the difference. The humility to admit your mistakes though it hurts your pride. And the perseverance to lift yourself up every time you fall.

You cannot find fulfilment without pursuing excellence. The callous approach to life may avoid the pain of exertion, but it leaves you unfulfilled. You are a part of the all-perfect God, and your soul naturally seeks to do something glorious. **When you exert yourself to be your best and do your best, then you experience the inner fulfilment your soul seeks.**

How can we cultivate a mindset of excellence? There is no blanket answer to this. However, here are some ways you can adopt to develop this mindset.

Take responsibility. This means holding yourself accountable for your actions, behaviours and attitudes in every situation. Though it may be easier to blame external circumstances or people, the willingness to take responsibility puts you in charge of yourself and urges you to make better decisions. Excellence naturally follows.

YOU HAVE SPELT 'RESUME' INCORRECTLY AND YOU SAY YOU GRADUATED IN ENGLISH MAJOR?

Keep raising the bar. To be satisfied with your present achievement means you have stopped growing. Instead, be grateful for what you have accomplished, but not satisfied. Commit yourself to higher goals and vision. Think, 'How can I serve to a greater extent? How can my abilities benefit more people?'

Embrace continuous improvement. The Japanese are known worldwide for the high quality of goods they produce. They have a term, 'kaizen', which has helped them win their international reputation for reliable quality. The term means 'continuous improvement' or 'change for the better'.

The kaizen theory states that you must constantly improve all areas of your life—professional, relational and societal. So, every time you do something, think how you can do it better next time. This attitude results in continuous incremental improvement.

Deliver beyond the basics. Fulfilling your job requirements is nothing special. Everyone does it. Employees who deliver the basics of their job are common. If you wish to be outstanding, you must look to deliver far greater value.

This does not mean taking on more commitments than you can deliver. Instead, it means to anticipate future needs. To go out of the way to accommodate requests. To help others with their tasks. And to bring ideas for improvement. This will undoubtedly set you apart from others and make you a valued asset in any field of work.

Do not try to master everything. There is a phrase for it: 'Jack of all trades, master of none.' It refers to those who acquire many skills but fail to achieve expertise in any. Today, this generalist versus specialist dichotomy has a more positive connotation.

It is important to possess a diverse skill set. It helps you be adaptable, versatile and innovative. On the other hand, expertise in your area of speciality is even more valuable. That is what produces the biggest impact. It results in quality work. People trust experts, not generalists. They want to work for experts and are motivated to learn from them. So, you must focus on deep learning and practise to become an expert in your chosen discipline.

In today's dynamic and complex environment, you will benefit from both expertise and generality. Therefore, balance the two to bring merit and finesse to your work.

54

Develop Your Leadership Abilities

Climbing atop Mount Everest, the world's highest mountain peak, is never free from perils. Once, many members and Sherpa guides of an ill-fated expedition died in the attempt. After the calamity, a surviving guide was asked on TV, 'Why do you put your life at stake in a profession where death is ever so close?'

The Sherpa responded, 'Being a mountain guide is dangerous. However, the satisfaction of taking others to the top is so thrilling, it is its own reward.'

Leaders are like mountain guides—they help others get to the top.

Why you should learn the art of leadership. Because good leadership always makes a difference. It galvanizes teams, turns around organizations, uplifts nations and transforms the world. As a leader, you get the opportunity to mould the future of people and projects. You set meaningful goals and chart out best strategies. You inspire followers to higher levels of excellence and support them in the face of challenges.

Difference between managers and leaders. Managers are not always leaders; they are followed because of their organizational position, even though they may be disliked by their subordinates. Likewise, leaders are not necessarily managers; their authority stems from the love and respect their followers have for them. At a typical workplace, managers focus on the process—they ensure things get done as required. On the other hand, leaders focus on people—they mentor, train and support people to get things done. They bring out the best in people.

Many a time in life, you are called upon to lead. By responding to such opportunities, you help others achieve success and fulfilment, and in the process, you experience the highest self-growth. The art of leadership is not an easy one to learn. But if you dedicate time and energy to mastering this fine skill, you will become a better person yourself and multiply your impact in your life and work. Hence, it is worthwhile to discuss salient attributes of good leaders, and how to develop them in ourselves.

Provide an inspiring vision for the future. As a leader, you must paint a worthy and convincing picture of where the team is headed. Only when they see a goal that is worthwhile, will they work hard to achieve it.

However, showing your team members the target ahead will also not suffice. Human nature is to forget and get disillusioned. A project may get off to a good start, but in the implementation phase, hiccups naturally happen. People tend to lose focus and become demotivated. As a leader, you must ensure you sustain their enthusiasm. To do so, you will have to restate the goals again and again, tell inspiring stories and keep the momentum going.

Be enthusiastic. The universal quality of good leaders is immense passion for their work. In fact, leadership in a team naturally gravitates to the individual who is most enthusiastic about accomplishing the common objectives.

When you are highly inspired about your job and enjoy it, your motivation infects others. This is essential because your key assignment as a leader is to get people to accomplish tasks.

Become expert in your field. Leaders win credibility easily when they have 'expert power'. If your people perceive you as the authority on a subject, they will not hesitate to follow your guidance and heed your advice. So, work hard to master your subject, for in doing so, you will also acquire the confidence to direct others.

Lead by example. Jim Kouzes and Barry Posner conducted a survey of 1,500 top executives in 20 countries.[20] They concluded that the quality subordinates wish to see most in CEOs is ethics. You must not merely give directives and make speeches but also win the respect of your team members by embodying the qualities they revere. Ralph Waldo Emerson expressed it aptly: 'What you do speaks so loudly that I cannot hear what you say.'

Followers wish to look up to role models they can emulate. They will gladly listen and dedicate themselves to leaders in whom they see the qualities they idolize. But if, they ever become convinced that you are not worthy of their respect, you can bid your leadership goodbye.

---

[20]Hill, Jessica, 'The Leadership Challenge: Four Qualities of a Leader That Motivate Others', *N Business*, 21 December 2014, https://bit.ly/3xwEIzF. Accessed on 15 June 2022.

Be patient and forbearing. While leading a team, many instances arise that test your tolerance and challenge your patience. After all, people are only human. They make mistakes, lose interest and sometimes become insincere. If you fly into a rage or flare up, you do not deserve to be in charge of them. Remember, **working with people is like polishing uncut diamonds—it takes time, repetition and patience to make them sparkle.**

HOW ELSE HAVE YOU DEMONSTRATED LEADERSHIP BESIDES GAINING 200 FOLLOWERS ON FACEBOOK?

Servant Leadership. To be a good leader, you must respect your people and care for their needs. This service attitude wins the trust of followers. You must mentor and support your team members like parents nurture their children. Once they are convinced you have their best interests at heart, they will enthusiastically follow your authority.

Poor leaders pursue personal agendas. They do not empathize with the needs of their people. Playing king of the hill, they pursue personal aggrandizement. However, people soon realize their impure intention and lose trust. And without trust, the house of leadership collapses like a deck of cards.

So, the first step in learning leadership is to develop *sevā* bhav towards those you wish to lead. You must desire to help them fulfil their aspirations and manifest their potential. Modern management science has only recently discovered the concept of 'servant leadership'. However, the Vedic civilization always emphasized service as the basis of statecraft.

Chandragupta Maurya was a famous king and a pivotal figure in Indian history about 2,000 years ago. He unified most of ancient India into one powerful kingdom and recaptured the various Greek kingdoms that had come up in the northwestern part of ancient India as the legacy of Alexander's invasion. He became so powerful that the Greek rulers receded before his might.

Chandragupta once asked his spiritual preceptor, 'Gurudev! As per the Vedas, what is the position of the king with respect to his subjects?'

His legendary guru, Chanakya Pandit, responded, 'The king is the servant of his people, and nothing more.'

The same idea has now found recognition in leadership science. Author Dale Galloway summed it up very well, 'The growth and development of people is the highest calling of a leader.'

To promote the cause of leadership, JKYog runs the Swami Mukundananda Leadership Academy (SMLA), which conducts varieties of workshops, seminars and training sessions for organizations. Learn about the various courses offered by the academy at *https://sm-leadership.org/*

In conclusion, the art of leadership is one of the finest skills you can learn. People do a lot for money; they do even more for values they deeply believe in, but they gladly dedicate their life for the leader who inspires the best in them. So, aim to grow your leadership qualities. Then, you will multiply your effectivity at work and relish the joy of helping others do the same.

55

Stay Focused in a Distracted World

Multitasking is the norm in modern workplaces. Has it happened to you that you are working on a complex report and your colleague messages you? You take your attention away from the report to chat with him for a couple of minutes and then return to the report. But by now you are thinking about what your colleague just told you. You take some time to regain your focus on the report, and *ping*, you receive an email alert from your boss. Now, your boss wants you to immediately respond to an irate customer. So, you drop the report and shift all your energy and attention to resolving the customer issue. At the end of the day, you look at your to-do list and realize you did not get this important report done! You put out a lot of fires, but the things that really mattered did not get done. That is the plight of most modern-day professionals.

Staying focused in a distracted world has become increasingly difficult. Our attention is being pulled in multiple directions at all times. We are constantly switching our focus between emails, text messages, phone calls, urgent requests and other demands. As a result, we feel exhausted, distracted and stressed at the end of the day. That makes us wonder whether there is a better way of doing things?

The concept of 'attention residue'. You may not realize it, but you are paying a huge price for the simple distractions at work and in life. Professor Sophie Leroy of University of Washington Bothell introduced the concept of 'attention residue'.[21] It explains that the brain struggles to switch between tasks. While switching from task 1 to task 2, part of your attention remains with the former instead of fully transferring to the next one. This 'attention residue' impedes your focus on the work at hand.

The residue is even thicker when you do not complete one task before moving on to another. The distracted mind brings down your overall productivity. It decreases your cognitive awareness, and you find it harder to get things done. Research has found that constant distractions at work lead to increased stress and reduced performance.

While managing workplace distractions is not fully in your control, there are some things you can do to regain focus. You can make simple choices every day that will help you limit distractions, so that you can get more things done with less stress.

Don't be a slave to technology, master it. This means to lessen the digital clutter you are exposed to, and instead, give attention to things that really add to the quality of life. It is easy to drown in the slurry of messages, texts and alerts. If you allow them to, they will drain your valuable time. Hence, be intentional and selective in how you use technology.

---

[21]Kelley, Peter, 'Task interrupted: A plan for returning helps you move on', UW News, 16 January 2018, https://bit.ly/3Rl1m7v. Accessed on 25 June 2022.

The only way to not get consumed by digital communication tools is to turn them off for some time in the day. Now, that may sound too extreme for some. If so, then another option is to digitally minimize by cutting out low-value apps and unsubscribing from all unnecessary groups, newsletters and mailing lists. You can manage notifications, and also send fewer emails and messages. Further, you can simplify home screens to stop the lure of browsing unnecessarily, by disconnecting them from news, updates, and the like.

Learn to say 'No'. Somebody will always come up with urgent requests for your time. Evaluate if it needs an immediate response. If not, learn to politely say 'No' and get back to it when you can.

Also, learn to say 'No' to requests for mindless gossip and unnecessary tea breaks. Watercooler conversations help build relations at work, but they often come at the cost of your focus and productivity. There are people who spend hours socializing at work and then scramble to get things done at the end of the day, oftentimes putting in late hours to meet deadlines. You can avoid this by staying disciplined and learning to politely say 'No'.

Timebox your schedule. Timeboxing is a technique that can help you stay focused on one thing at a time. It means to divide your schedule into fixed blocks of time for specific tasks. For example, three hours for an urgent complex task, 30 minutes for research for a project, 45 minutes for communication and 30 minutes for reporting. This keeps you accountable for time and in control of your schedule. It adds time pressure, but in a motivating way.

Build focus hours in your workday. Find one to two hours of uninterrupted and focused time on your daily calendar. This may be early in the morning before your alerts start ringing or at the end of the day. During this time, you get your most important tasks done—the ones that are complex and cognitively demanding. This includes allocating a specified location to work uninterruptedly. Determining the amount of time per task. Setting rules for social media and chit-chats. And resisting breaks by keeping all resources at hand.

There is a saying: 'You cannot do big things if you are distracted by small things.' Today, 'focus' is called the currency of modern economy. Distractions are abundant, but people who are able to remain focused in a distracted world are the ones who make progress and build the careers they envision.

56

Dealing with a Bad Boss

It is often said that people do not quit companies, they quit bad bosses. Turnover is an acute problem in the corporate world. Research says that ineffective managers are the primary cause of it. Inept bosses compel good employees to leave due to their bad attitude, tendency to micromanage and negligence.

While bad bosses impact a company's productivity and profit and loss statement (P&L), they also deeply impact an individual's mental and physical health. A Swedish survey of more than 3,000 employees found that among those who work for toxic bosses, 60 per cent were more likely to suffer a stroke, heart attack or other life-threatening cardiac conditions.[22] Employees with bad bosses are also more prone to stress, anxiety and depression.

There are many kinds of bosses, but two that you should distinguish between. There are tough bosses who challenge you and raise the bar for your performance, and are invested in your career growth. They may not be easy to work with because of

---

[22]Abbajay, Mary, 'What to Do When You Have a Bad Boss', *Harvard Business Review*, 7 September 2018, https://bit.ly/2NmtGIv. Accessed 25 June 2022.

their high standards, but you trust their support and stand to gain in the long run.

Then there is the other kind—the bad bosses who negatively impact your life in many ways. They publicly humiliate you, throw fits of anger or do not give you the credit and recognition you deserve. They are definitely not invested in your personal and professional growth. These are the bad bosses we will learn to deal with in this chapter.

If you have a bad boss, here are some things you can do instead of suffering every day.

See what is in your control. If you are dealing with a toxic boss and you have had enough, do an analysis of the situation, and see if you can quit your job and move to another company. Or perhaps, change your job or team within the same company. If that is not an option, see if there is any way to provide feedback about the boss or address the situation by sharing it with a skip level manager or the HR department.

These options may often not be available. Regardless, you should continue to use ways that are within your control.

Do not make this personal. Bad bosses have a special knack for demeaning people and making it very personal. The employee on the receiving end often takes the feedback personally, which sabotages their confidence and morale. If you have identified that your boss has low emotional intelligence, makes harsh comments or harps excessively on mistakes, realize that it is the boss's problem, not yours. They are perhaps projecting their fears, shortcomings and insecurities onto you.

Therefore, understand your part in the situation—learn from your mistakes but do not personalize everything. You cannot change what they say, but you can change how you react to it. Do not emotionally entangle yourself with every remark—remain detached and keep your peace of mind.

Have the courage to speak up. If your boss bullies you, speak up. Here is what will happen. Either the boss will fire you, or they will learn that you are not a pushover, so they'll never do that again. To stand up to your boss or to speak up when needed can seem daunting to many people. But speaking up and setting boundaries can be a big step in your attempt to improve things. Read the chapter 'Establish Boundaries in Relationships' for more wisdom on the topic.

Your job is not your life. These days, jobs are seen as the all in all of one's identity and life. People sacrifice health and relationships to keep their job. So, it is only natural that they get obsessed with everything related to their job, including their boss.

It is important to remember that the situation with your boss is temporary. The purpose of your life is greater than just pleasing your boss. Therefore, no matter what happens at work, take time for other activities that nurture you.

Keep a spiritual perspective. It is said that God sends us the people we need, not the people we want. Some people are placed in our lives to help us grow in patience, humility and empathy. All of these qualities are virtues that help us in the spiritual journey.

When you are dealing with a bad boss, it is extremely hard to keep a spiritual perspective and see God seated in that person's heart. But all the saints who had deep devotion, exemplified that no matter how people treated them, they always maintained their equanimity and felt the presence of God in everyone. We cannot reach that elevated state in a moment, but we can certainly try a little every day.

57

Overcoming Career Setbacks

Career setbacks can come in many forms: you did not get the job you wanted or the promotion you deserved, your project failed or you were fired. These can be shattering situations; everyone experiences some kind of setback in their careers. Even some of the world's most successful people have gone through this pain.

Steve Jobs was fired from the very company he founded, Apple.

Jack Ma, the billionaire founder of Alibaba, applied for 30 different jobs and got rejected in each one of them. He applied for a job at KFC, a fast food chain, where 24 people applied, and everyone was selected except him.

Career setbacks come with shock, denial, self-doubt and anger. For example, an employee who just lost their job not only has to find another job but also deal with self-doubt, sadness and frustration. Since jobs are such an important part of people's lives, career setbacks make them feel a loss of identity and purpose.

Though they can be devastating, it is not the end of the world. As said in a *Harvard Business Review* article, 'Even a dramatic career failure can become a springboard to success if you respond in the right way.'[23]

Here are some ways to handle career setbacks with resilience.

Understand why the debacle happened. When a career setback occurs and a person starts to process it, they can start blaming themselves and completely sabotage their self-confidence. Or, they can blame others and absolve themselves of responsibility for what happened.

The problem with both the reactions is that business decisions are not always based on a person's performance. Instead, they could be related to the company's strategic direction, restructuring, mergers, acquisitions or economic downturns, among other things. Consequently, it is not right to squarely blame yourself and feel a loss of self-worth. Nor does it help to blame others, since such corporate decisions depend on many factors.

Therefore, it is important to step back and understand why this happened to you. If possible, reach out to the key decision-makers and ask for feedback on what you could have done to prevent it. For example, if you did not get a promotion, ask your manager for the reasons behind the decision. If you want to receive honest feedback, then do it with an intent to understand, not to confirm your accusations of injustice or to seek a reversal of the verdict.

Take action. Instead of wallowing in self-pity, take steps to

[23]Lee Marks, Mitchell, et al., 'Rebounding from Career Setbacks', *Harvard Business Review*, October 2014, https://bit.ly/3wlyoeB. Accessed on 15 June 2022.

bounce back. You will probably not find another job or get promoted in a day, so focus on doing simple things every day that will help you rebound. If you are looking for a job, start by updating your resume. Publish it on online job portals. Reach out to a career counsellor. Connect with your network and speak to friends. Further, show willingness to learn new skills if that helps you get a new job or promotion. Volunteer at a non-profit to diversify your skill set and network. This can seem frustrating, so you will need patience and resilience through this period.

Assess the situation. Many people look at career setbacks as an opportunity to ask tough questions: 'Am I really doing what I want to do?' For example, a person got fired from a marketing job because he failed to meet the sales quota. He was frustrated on losing his job and income, but after some self-reflection, he realized he never quite enjoyed being a salesman. So, he looked at this setback as an opportunity to change his profession.

Sometimes, people reflect on their priorities in life. A person was neglecting her health for her work. On losing the high-paying stressful job, she realized it will help her restore work-life balance. Now, she has more time to prioritize health and family.

Like all other setbacks in life, it is important to keep a spiritual perspective in career setbacks as well. Those with faith in God always try to see His grace in every situation. This helps them sail through the highs and lows of life. They learn the lessons, improve themselves and move forward with renewed vigour.

58

Ride the Waves of Workplace Politics

Workplace politics often conjures up images of people fighting and stabbing each other to finish at the top of the race. People think you should either stay miles away from politics or be in the thick of it to get what you want. Let us understand why workplace politics happens in the first place.

In any workplace or organization, there is an interplay of limited resources and people come with different ambitions, needs and emotions. This results in power play. To reach desired goals, people have to influence others for which they deploy different tactics.

Politics is a reality in every organization. It is best to find ways to deal with it without compromising your personal and professional values.

Learn to navigate. You are in your organization for a reason and that is to get your job done in the most effective and efficient manner. To be successful, be cognizant of how your company or establishment functions. How do people interact with each other? How does work get done? Who are the key decision makers, and what gets rewarded? This will help you navigate the organizational structure, informal networks and power dynamics.

For example, you want to launch a project which needs funding approval from a leader other than your boss. This project is not the biggest priority for that leader. So, how do you influence her to fund your project? You do not have to deploy any shady tactics for it. Instead, you can do this in a straightforward manner by building a rapport and communicating persuasively, supported with credible data. If you come across as sincere, it will help develop your reputation.

SIR, I CAN ASSURE YOU, I LOVE TEAMWORK!
I JUST HATE MY TEAMMATES

Build your network. At the centre of politics are people. Building connections with people will help you understand them. So, establish healthy relationships, where you learn how you can help others and they can help you. Find out what drives other people, so you can find common interests and collectively achieve the goals of the organization.

Be the change you want to see. If there is any aspect of your workplace culture that you despise, then have the courage to change it. For example, if you do not like your teammates gossiping about others, then do not be party to it. If you do not like credit being taken away, then give others credit when it is due.

Be respectful and nice. Take it as a personal challenge to maintain your cool and be respectful and courteous at all times. If you are able to maintain your cool even in provocative situations, you will be able to disentangle from petty office politics and remain stress free. In fact, **if you genuinely want to grow from within, our scriptures teach us to give respect to others and not expect it for ourselves.** This humble position allows us to be unaffected by politics.

Do not play favourites. People, especially in power, like to play favourites, which creates a lot of tension in teams and workplaces. If you are a boss, avoid playing favourites—treat everyone equally. Do not draw comparisons publicly, as this makes people feel insecure and react in negative ways.

Always be fair. There are times when you cannot avoid getting dragged into a difficult game of office politics. In such cases, be fair in your words and actions. Avoid judgement by addressing the unjust behaviour, not the individual. Focus on the issue at hand and solve it with facts and results. Resist pointing fingers or playing the blame game.

Forgive and forget. Do not hold grudges against people as it only makes your own life miserable. Try to address the issue you have with the person, so you both can move on and forge better relations in the future.

Accept. It is important to acknowledge and accept office politics as a part of the workplace. It is inevitable and the sooner you acquiesce to this notion, the sooner you will move on from it. You may not agree with it, but you can learn to live with it for the sake of your sanity.

59

Improve Your Emotional Quotient (EQ)

During the first-half of the twentieth century, Intelligence Quotient (IQ) was considered a singular measure of one's abilities. It could be likened to the horsepower of an engine, which tells how powerful it is. Therefore, IQ tests were the determining criteria in job selection processes. However, as the saying goes: 'It takes more than intelligence to act intelligently.'

Over the last four decades, research has revealed that a high IQ is no predictor of success. People could be technically brilliant, but if they are unable to manage their emotions, work in teams and handle adversity, their chances of success are limited.

This discovery led to growing interest in the concept of 'Emotional Intelligence'. The term was introduced by Daniel Goleman in his paper published in the *Harvard Business Review* in 1998, based on his study of executives from 200 organizations. The paper established that the performance of organizations was directly correlated to the EQ of managers.

What is EQ? It involves three things: 1) awareness of your own emotions, 2) ability to manage your emotions, and 3) empathy for the emotions of others.

EQ is the ability to recognize and understand both your own emotions and those of others around you. People with high emotional intelligence are self-aware. They regulate their moods. They empathize with others and use that awareness to guide their decisions. This makes them respond, not react, to problems. They become known for their ability to diffuse conflict in the workplace, to remain resilient through challenges and solve complex problems. It is not surprising that emotional intelligence is linked to higher salaries and greater job satisfaction.

Goleman expressed it well, 'CEOs get hired for their business expertise and intelligence but get fired for their lack of emotional intelligence.' Even when professionals who have similar technical skills and intelligence are compared, EQ accounts for 90 per cent of what gets people promoted within an organization.

Unfortunately, we learnt mathematics, science and history in school, but nobody taught us how to manage emotions. We do not even realize its importance until we are thrown into situations where our emotional intelligence is tested.

For example, when a brilliant employee is promoted to a management position, suddenly she finds it difficult to manage people. She is always frustrated with her team, gets annoyed when people ask questions and cannot motivate others. She possesses the required technical expertise but lacks the emotional awareness.

People's EQ is influenced by their socialization, upbringing and beliefs. The rest can be developed through learning and practise. The tips listed below should be studied in-depth and then practised in everyday life.

Practise self-awareness. Self-awareness is the ability to recognize and understand your own emotions and how they affect your performance. It is the keystone of emotional intelligence.

For example, do you automatically feel jealous every time another colleague is praised? Do you start thinking negative thoughts about yourself or do you start belittling the colleague? Instead of drowning in jealousy and suffering, the first step is to proactively become aware of that emotion. Think of past experiences when you have reacted the same way emotionally.

Regulate your emotions. It is critical to be able to control your moods and impulses, rather than be controlled by them. Let us say, you have an important presentation to make, and you are feeling nervous. People with high EQ will realize that it is only natural to feel nervous. Instead of letting these emotions overtake them, they regulate and control them. They focus their attention on preparing for the presentation, learning the content and anticipating questions that might come up.

Empathize. This is the ability to understand others, their needs and viewpoints. Emotionally intelligent people avoid forming stereotypes, and instead, listen intently. They read non-verbal cues to understand what the other person is going through. Consequently, they also have better relationships.

People with high EQ are able to sustain their inspiration even in the face of adversity. They control their emotions and then motivate themselves to do what they need to do. They are also experts at finding the silver lining in unfavourable situations, so they remain positive.

Considering all these benefits, prioritize the development of a high EQ, and take steps to achieve it.

60

Find a Mentor

Whether you want to move ahead professionally, or you wish to launch a successful start-up, you will benefit tremendously from a mentor. Studies reveal that 75 per cent of all successful executives ascribe mentoring as a key to their accomplishments.[24]

Those who receive mentoring are five times more likely to be promoted than others (Gartner 2006).[25] Therefore, one of the biggest factors in career growth is the presence of a good mentor.

Who are mentors? The dictionary defines them as 'wise and trusted advisors'. In the professional world, such advisors could be higher-ups in the organization or successful businesspersons.

Mentors are people who have 'been there and done that'. Hence, they possess wisdom gained from years of experience. Most importantly, they are willing, and even eager, to share their

---

[24]Newman, Stephen, 'Hey, Coach!', *td magazine*, 1 March 2019, https://bit.ly/2TlDQrG. Accessed on 25 June 2022.
[25]Knowledge at Wharton, 'Workplace Loyalties Change but the Value of Mentoring Doesn't', 16 May 2007, https://whr.tn/2MawI3d. Accessed on 25 June 2022.

expertise with you. Therefore, they become your one-stop resource for invaluable experience that would otherwise have taken you ages to accumulate.

The path to accomplishment is never an easy one, and we do not always have the answer to every challenge that comes our way. In the face of difficulties, mentors provide us support, hope and encouragement. They save us from costly mistakes and years of fumbling. They help us set measurable goals and impose the self-discipline necessary to achieve them.

The personal coaching we receive from mentors is priceless. Having succeeded themselves, they altruistically offer a little bit of their time for one-on-one guidance. With their abundant experience, they see our shortcomings—which are often not visible to us—and point out the areas in which we need improvement. Hence, in any career path, receiving mentorship becomes one of the most formidable ways to leapfrog ahead.

Qualities of mentors. Nowadays, corporations and educational establishments often have institutionalized mentoring programmes. In fact, 71 per cent of Fortune 500 corporations invest in personal counselling systems.[26] Hence, you may come across opportunities to receive mentorship, either as a formalized process or informally. In this scenario, it is important to know how to find a good mentor. Here are some qualities to look for when you search for your personal coach.

- **Good mentors are role models.** Since we see them as ideals, we are inspired to emulate them. Modelling our

[26]Ibid.

mentor is a potent way to develop skills, character and personality.

- **Good mentors are experts.** No matter what our area of learning, guides can be helpful only to the extent that they are thorough in the subject. Hence, good mentors should be experts in their field who are willing to liberally share life lessons and their expertise with us.

- **Good mentors are accessible.** They provide us personal tutoring. If you are a junior executive, the CEO of your company will not be your ideal guide, since you only get to meet him once a year. An ideal mentor is one who is approachable and also has the patience and time to listen to you.

- **Good mentors are kind and helpful.** They care for us and have genuine interest in our success. By their warmth and selflessness, we are encouraged to look to them as our friends and supporters. They are trustworthy because they are not in it for themselves.

- **Good mentors have high integrity.** You can share your woes and struggles with them, knowing you will not be betrayed. Their trustworthiness assures you that the advice they offer is for your best interests, not theirs.

In conclusion, an expert guide and caring personal coach is one of the biggest blessings in life. We should proactively strive to find a good mentor for ourselves.

61

Manage Your Time Well

R am and Shyam graduated from college and started their jobs at the same company at the same time. Within 10 years, Ram was promoted to a senior management position, whereas Shyam struggled to keep his job. Why?

In the same period of 10 years, both invested their time differently. Ram used the time to learn, work on important projects and consistently deliver value. On the other hand, Shyam squandered his time in office politics, low-value activities and complaining about his boss. How they spent their time created such a vast difference in their lives.

Many suggestions in this book require using the resource of time. But unfortunately, time is a finite resource that constantly keeps passing away. Every day we wake up, receive the same 1,440 minutes to utilize or waste away. Effective people put the minutes to good use. They take charge of every single moment of the day and get the maximum return on it.

In contrast, ineffective people dissipate their time on trivial matters. By the end of the day, things remain undone, and they find they are no closer to their goal. Therefore, implementation of the suggestions in this book requires learning to utilize the consumable resource of time judiciously to achieve our personal, societal and professional goals.

The principle of time management applies to all fields. The scriptures state: *kshaṇasaḥ kshaṇaso vidyā, kaṇasaḥ kaṇaso dhanam* 'It is by saving single pennies that people become billionaires. And it is by using individual moments to accumulate knowledge that one becomes a scholar.'

The question is: how do we invest every minute wisely? Below are some time management secrets of successful people like Warren Buffett, Bill Gates and others. See how you can practise these in your life.

We make time for what we prioritize. Do you plan your week's activities and include reading a book, spending time with the children or preparing for a marathon but are unable to find time for them by the week's end? Do you complain to yourself, 'I really wanted to, but I was too busy...'

The truth is you were not too busy; you just did not prioritize those activities. Imagine if one of your children fell sick. No matter how busy your schedule, you would take out the time to care for them. It is simple—if you think it is important enough, you will make the time for it.

The problem is that we fail to understand what is really important. **Poor priorities lead to poor time management.**

Warren Buffett's pilot, Michael 'Mike' Flint, who flew him for many years, told a story. Once on a flight, Buffett asked Michael to list down 25 things he wanted to do in life over the next five years. After Michael had put together his list, Buffett asked him to review it again and select the top five most important things.

Michael was hesitant because everything on the list to him was important. However, since Buffett insisted, he came back with his list of top five. Buffett then asked Michael when he would start working on this list of top five things. Michael did not want to waste any time, so he said he would start immediately.

Then he asked Buffett what he should do with the remaining list of 20 important things. To which Buffett replied, 'Nothing, everything you didn't circle should be avoided at all costs. Don't do them until you've succeeded in the top five.'

Pareto's Principle. This famous principle is also known as the 80/20 rule. It states that 20 per cent of our actions drive 80 per cent of our results. While there are hundreds of things you could do every day, 20 per cent of them are responsible for the maximum return in the form of happiness, well-being, health or anything else you aim to achieve. Likewise, 80 per cent of your actions contribute only 20 per cent towards your goals.

The trick in time management is to identify the 20 per cent activities that count the most. Focus and invest your time on these most important items and eliminate or reduce all other demands on your schedule.

To-do lists help to remember what is important. You have identified what is important for you, but the next challenge is to turn these abstract ideas and goals into reality. For example, if you plan to author a book, breaking it down into small actionable tasks and putting them in daily, weekly and monthly to-do lists will make this daunting project seem more achievable.

Do the important work, not the easy work. It is gratifying to strike items off your to-do list after completing them. The only problem is that people like to do the easy and unimportant tasks first, while they postpone the important but difficult ones for later. Consequently, they get the satisfaction of scoring off an item from their to-do list, although factually, it does not count for much.

Brian Tracy expressed it beautifully in his book, *Eat That Frog.*[27] The frog is that one task on your to-do list which is difficult, and you lack the motivation to do. But if you finish it, everything else on your to-do list will become much easier. He suggests you start the day by tackling the frog. Tracy's strategy is also the one taught by management consultants.

However, why limit yourself to tackling the frog first thing in the morning? Why not tackle your frog at every moment of the day? Let me share my personal time management strategy here.

People ask how I am able to calmly take care of the innumerable demands on my time while leading the JKYog worldwide mission that includes a hundred organizations in its fold.

I tell them, 'It is really quite simple. I know I cannot do the hundreds of things that come up before me every day. So, I keep the goals and priorities at the back of my mind. And at every moment, I ask myself, "What is the most important thing I could do now?" Then I go ahead and do it, whether it is guiding a new

---

[27]Tracy, Brian, *Eat That Frog!: 21 Great Ways to Stop Procrastinating and Get More Done in Less Time*, Berrett-Koehler Publishers; 3rd edition (2017).

project, addressing a managerial issue, solving a devotee's problem or self-rejuvenating.'

Ultimately, that is the best anyone can do, isn't it? To pick upon the most important task in the moment—while remaining aware of the larger goals—and focus on doing it well. This strategy also gives me the flexibility to adjust to any important demands that may crop up from moment to moment.

Much more could be said on the topic of time management. But let this much suffice for the scope of this book. The next article delves into time management techniques that will help you maximize productivity at work and also free your time for things that you enjoy most.

62

How to Achieve Work-Life Balance

Gone are the days when people would punch in for work at 9 a.m. and out at 5 p.m. Today, work takes precedence over much of our lives. Long hours, increasing demands, working across time zones and the pressure to stay connected with technology have become the norm.

But they come at a heavy cost. We invest more time and effort at work at the expense of other aspects of our life such as physical, mental, social and spiritual well-being. The fine line between work and home life has been obliterated in much of society, disrupting work-life balance.

However, such a life is lopsided and devoid of quality. It is neither sustainable in the long run, nor satisfying to your soul. If you wish to lead a quality life, you must learn to find some way to balance its important aspects.

What is work-life balance? While it would be ideal to spend equal time at work and home, such a notion is rarely the case. The right balance for you will vary based on your context— whether you are single, married, have children, are starting out in your career, nearing retirement, etc. There is no perfect, one-size-fits-all solution that applies to everyone.

Balance simply implies that all aspects of your life are in check—work satisfaction, familial happiness, physical fitness and internal growth. If not, then disharmony at work and home becomes the cause of major discontentment, discord in relationships and ill health.

Hence, to be happy and more productive, you must learn to achieve equilibrium between work and life. Let us first look at how we can attain balance at work.

Prioritize your responsibilities. It is essential to have your workplace priorities in order. Figure out which responsibilities cannot be compromised and which are flexible. What are your most important commitments at work, for yourself as well as for the organization? Which tasks require excellence and perfection, and which merely need to be finished? Having clarity on these answers will help you utilize your time and effort in alignment with your priorities.

Plan your day. You can divide your workday in various ways. It should include activities for the day, the time you end your work and the evening ahead. You can allocate action items to complete in the first-half of your workday before lunch, and others for the second half. Then do your best to leave work by the 'end time' that you or the organization has set. The latter part of your day is now free to spend with family and engage in activities that will add to your life quality.

Establish boundaries. To be productive both at work and home, you must set fair and realistic limits on what you will and will not do. Equally important is to communicate these to your managers, colleagues and family. For instance, commit to working late only in emergency situations or where deadlines are being compromised.

Similarly, have a set time at home when you do not respond to work-related emails or phone calls. For example, do not pick up the phone while having dinner with the family or going for an evening walk with your spouse. Further, evaluate your family schedule before saying 'Yes' to additional responsibilities.

You can also open up to your boss and ask for support and flexible working arrangements to maintain work-life balance. These could include job-sharing, back-up support of team members or working from home. I have dealt with this topic in detail in the chapter 'Establish Boundaries in Relationships'.

With these work-related techniques under your belt, you can now look at some personal self-care tools to achieve work-life harmony.

Unplug. Office work must not be allowed to encroach upon your weekends, evening time with family or temple satsang. To unplug from office, do not respond to work-related emails and phone calls during 'off' hours. By all means, be present for a crisis but make it an exception.

Schedule your personal activities. While it is important to leave work at work, one of the ways to accomplish it is by scheduling your personal pursuits. It is said that what gets scheduled, gets done. So, if vacations and family time are scheduled, there is a greater chance you will make time for them.

Keep time for personal development. Your emotional, intellectual and spiritual growth contribute to your success in life. Hence, taking time out for meditation, reading or other self-improvement pursuits is very necessary. This gives clarity to your thoughts and the ability to respond appropriately when situations present themselves.

I am reminded of the famous adage: 'All work and no play makes Jack a dull boy.' Hopefully, this chapter has given you a few insights into achieving a healthy work-life balance.

63

Managing Work-Related Stress

Today, an overwhelming number of working professionals report feeling overly pressured. With so many demands and expectations, work can wreak havoc on your well-being. While it is normal to experience short-term pressure of meeting deadlines, long-term stress is exceedingly harmful. It can adversely affect both your physical and mental health.

Common work-related stressors. People experience stress at work for various reasons. Some of these are: unrealistic expectations, lack of sufficient skills for the job and frequent conflicts. Add to that lack of job security, poor advancement opportunities and late office hours, and you now have a recipe for stress.

Damaging effects of stress. Studies have shown that regular bouts of stress-related chemicals, such as cortisol, epinephrine and norepinephrine can have disastrous effects. It can result in increased risk of heart disease, high blood pressure, type 2 diabetes and insomnia. In dire situations, it can cause depression or prompt violent reactions, and in extreme cases, even suicide. Moreover, anxiety affects not only our body and mind but can also trickle into our home life and affect our relationships.

If you are facing the kind of work-related stress explained above, it is time to take action to manage it. To walk away from stressors at work would be ideal but not realistic. Here are some healthy ways to tackle stress that you may experience at work.

Organize yourself. We have covered some elements of this, including to-do lists, time management techniques and others. While you incorporate these tools, remember to also keep your desk organized and free of clutter. Make sure to have a healthy breakfast, plan for traffic on your way to work and reach work on time to maximize your day.

Do not aim to be a perfectionist. No matter how hard you try to do a thing perfectly, mistakes always creep in. If you are targeting perfection, then the tiniest errors will stress you. Therefore, strive for excellence, not perfection.

Apple co-founder, Steve Jobs, used to say: 'Some mistakes will be made along the way. That is good. Because some decisions are being made along the way. We'll find the mistakes. We'll fix them.' So, do not be afraid if a mistake happens. Have the courage to accept it, work to rectify it and try not to repeat it.

Take a break. Quick time away from the work desk can provide a well-needed pause. Consider calling up a trusted friend or a loved one during your five-minute break. Or perhaps, walk around and freshen up.

In addition to taking breaks during the workday, schedule time for occasional excursions and recreational activities outside of work. Go ahead and pursue your hobbies. You can then come to work feeling relaxed and ready to take on complex tasks.

The root cause of stress. Anxiety develops when we are attached to a particular outcome and are worried that things may not turn out as we desire.

School students often suffer stress near exams, not because of lack of talent, but because of attachment to the results. Similarly, some people lose their confidence when speaking to an audience, because of their desire to be liked and be called a great speaker. In both these cases, the mind is invested in the outcome. So, how do we effectively deal with this?

Focus on the process. Keeping your mind on the end goal can be overwhelming and intimidating. Instead, keep your attention on the process. Break down the bigger goal into smaller, more manageable tasks. Then do each bit with dedication.

For example, if you have a speech to deliver to an audience of a thousand people, do not just think about the end result or be overwhelmed by the enormity of the audience. Instead, focus on the writing, the content and the delivery. You will find the stress diminishing substantially.

Remember, God is the Enjoyer. Even if after all the effort you are unable to accomplish what you set out to, remember that you are not the enjoyer of the results. They are meant for the pleasure of God. If you can develop a spiritual perspective that you are a servant of God and He is the enjoyer of the fruits of your actions, you will not be depressed every time things do not go your way.

While we cannot eliminate stressors, we can learn to control our emotions and reactions to them. Finally, with wisdom and practise, we can eradicate stress from the root.

64

Being Productive While Working from Home

Working remotely has seen a tremendous rise over the years, making it the new-age mantra. And the Covid-19 pandemic has made working from home even more prevalent. It has created a paradigm shift of traditional work set-up to remote working. This book would, thus, have been incomplete without a guide to working from home (WFH).

With advancement in technology, teleworking has become a universally accepted practice. Remote work statistics (Owl Labs, 2022) inform us that 52 per cent of the world's employees work from home at least once every week, while 18 per cent work remotely full-time. Sixteen per cent of companies around the globe work entirely online.[28] These numbers are not going to downsize, rather, they will continue to grow in the coming years.

Benefits of WFH. Global remote work has been a win-win for both employees and organizations. Teleworkers have left behind

---

[28]Roshi, Ludjon, 'Remote Work Statistics in 2022: Facts About Telecommuting', *Codeless*, 5 June 2022, https://bit.ly/3wl754p. Accessed on 25 June 2022.

the long commutes and unhealthy outside meals. This has resulted in saving time and money, while adding convenience and physical wellness to their lives. Added benefits include flexible working hours and work-life balance that everyone desires. People have used this extra time to incorporate an exercise regime, spend more time with their families or simply introspect and discover greater meaning to life.

As a welcome additional benefit, remote work has had a transformational influence on a societal level. People are migrating to the suburbs and embracing the lower cost of living. And most noticeable is the extra time with family, friends and relatives.

Detriments of WFH. While teleworking seems like a perfect arrangement, there is the flip side to it. Remote working comes with a greater risk of mental health issues. A Qualtrics study of more than 2,000 employees in 2020 from various countries revealed that 41.6 per cent of the respondents experienced a deterioration in mental health since Covid-19.[29]

Burnout syndrome or chronic work-related stress has become a common phenomenon. Factors such as lack of sufficient breaks and blurred boundaries between work and home are the top stressors. Add to that increased distractions, lack of structure and relationship differences at home, and you have a recipe for disaster.

Working from home is, therefore, a mix of both good and bad,

---

[29]'The Other COVID-19 Crisis: Mental Health', *Qualtrics*, 14 April 2020, https://bit.ly/3b3sRlk. Accessed on 15 June 2022.

varying from person to person. Let me share some tips and tricks to help you perform your best and maintain your sanity while being a remote worker.

Create a routine. To feel productive, we must maintain structure and discipline. Now that you are no longer being watched, you'll have to push yourself to create an effective timetable. It will enable you to manage your time wisely and remain focused on work. Hence, be strict with yourself and follow a schedule.

Try to wake up at the same time each day to develop a routine. Likewise, lunch, too, should be at the same time every day. Include in your lunch hour a few minutes to unplug and recharge. Resist the urge of working through lunch.

Breaks from screen are absolutely essential for those working on computers all day. Health and safety regulations suggest taking a short 5–10 minute break every hour from Display Screen Equipment (DSE) to reduce risk of tired eyes and headaches.

Get up and stretch, look far outside the window or simply do some deep breathing exercises during this break. Opportunities for such breaks come naturally when working at the office. At home, you have to impose them upon yourself.

The End Of the Day (EOD) must also be scheduled if you want a sustainable work model. Have a timer that goes off by your desired EOD time. Try to adhere to it and leave work behind for the day.

Separate your home and workspace. It is important to have a dedicated workspace away from where the family relaxes or stays majority of the time. That means not working at the kitchen table or couch. This will help you focus on work during working hours. It will also allow you to shift away from work by closing it off at the end of the day. Try finding a cosy nook for yourself where you can shut out everything. Remain in your workspace while working and venture into the home space during breaks and at the end of the day.

Reduce meetings. Heard of Zoom burnout? Yes, many teleworkers attest to spending majority of their working day in meetings. However, most are unnecessary and can limit productive outputs. Yes, they are helpful as we initiate a project, but later, they eat valuable time. Execution is what matters after the long hours of planning—concentrate on that. So, before you accept a meeting, be clear on the agenda and context, evaluate the impact of your contribution, and feel free to say 'No'.

Practise self-care. Working from home gives you an opportunity to take better care of yourself and get replenished. Use the time you would spend commuting to engage in exercise. With the kitchen at your disposal, you can make quick and healthy meals.

Go outside and expose yourself to sunshine daily. It will uplift your mood and improve your health. Meditation breaks or quick power naps are additional ways of boosting both physical and mental health.

Maintain harmony in relationships at home. It's easy to get carried away with work when at home, taking family for granted. But this will backfire. Ensure dedicated quality time with spouse and children daily. Even if it is for 30 minutes, give them undivided attention and care. Share your schedule with the family to set the expectations ahead of time. Divide home chores to ease the extra load on family members. These practices will induce peace and happiness in relationships.

Another way this plays out is having too much association with others since everyone is under the same roof. This too is unhealthy as all need their 'Me time'—uninterrupted space and time. In this case, set boundaries. Agree to spend time together after work and keep talks and association during the day to a minimum. Communicate and adhere to rules of interruption so that they know when it's acceptable to engage with you and when not to do so. This will help keep you from getting on each other's nerves!

Working from home may be different but doesn't have to be hard. Though there may be challenges, we can always choose to look at them as opportunities. Working from home allows time with family that may have been missing earlier. It gives you a chance to improve your health and well-being. And instead of being outwardly oriented, being at home allows for time to go within—to spend time on introspection and self-improvement.

Section Five

FINANCIAL ABUNDANCE

65

The Secret to Earning Financial Wealth

Earning money is seen as a complex task. People who struggle with it look at the wealthy and wonder if they possess some special technique. This gives rise to the question: 'What is the secret to making lots of money?'

The answer is in fact so simple, it is contained in just two words: 'add value'. Providing benefit through your work is the most reliable way to earn more money. The reason is that the value you provide is inextricably linked to the compensation you receive. The more benefit you bring through your work, the more financially abundant your life will be. And this applies to all—whether you are an employee, a seller of goods or a provider of services.

Adding value versus working. There is a big difference between these two. If you dig a hole in your backyard garden, and later fill it up, you may have worked hard, but the value added is nil. No one has benefitted from it. Similarly, the purpose of employment is not to just log the required working hours; it is to add value to your company. Make 'add value' your goal, and you will also develop a heightened sense of purpose and passion.

Average work results in average wages. Most employees think of their work as a nine-to-five job for which they get paid. They do not pay attention to the benefit they are providing to their employer. They feel they need a raise but do not bother to think why they deserve it. Some go a step further—they do just sufficient work to ensure they are not fired. Then, they feel frustrated when they do not receive promotions, while others do.

However, the perspective of employers is obviously different. They evaluate the wages paid against the benefit received. Naturally, they offer more salary to employees who contribute more to their organization.

Adding value grows business. This simple truth often eludes business owners. Their singular goal becomes to maximize revenue from customers. But this becomes a short-sighted view of business. If customers do not receive sufficient benefit for the price paid, they do not return. And it ends up as a one-time sale.

Instead, if they had received amazing value, they would come back for more. And next time, they would even be willing to pay higher because of the excellent quality they got. Such an intention of the seller—to benefit the customer—ends up becoming a win-win for both.

Creating wealth. The simple rule of microeconomics 101 states that customers continue to purchase a commodity or service until the marginal value added is equal to the marginal cost they pay. At that point, it does not make sense to purchase any further. However, when customers perceive they are receiving greater value than the price paid, they continue to return for more.

Thus, the principle of a long-lasting and successful business is quite simple. **Wealth is created by serving and satisfying customers better than others do.**

See your work or business as an opportunity to solve problems of others and satisfy their needs. Make it your motto to help others to the extent that no one else can match. Look for ways to add value—to your customers, to your employer, to your colleagues and to your subordinates. Then, success and wealth will be a natural consequence.

66

Inculcate the Habit of Saving

In this age of consumption, the trend is to buy now and pay later. Almost everything, right from a home and car to shirts and trousers, are available on Equated Monthly Instalments, or EMI. This means that you pay for the expense over an extended period of time instead of at the time of purchase. While this seems to go well for some time, the problem starts when the cycle of life takes a turn and you lose your job, someone in the family gets sick, the economy enters a downturn or you face an unplanned financial loss.

With no regular income and no savings to fall back upon, the unpaid EMIs quickly pile up. The calls from collection agencies cause a huge amount of stress that affects every aspect of life. If you are unable to arrange the money, you might lose your favourite car and in extreme circumstances, even your home. Such an experience can break your confidence, making it difficult to rebuild your life once again.

You may say, 'This can never happen to me', but so did the people to whom it happened; they too had never thought it could happen to them. Therefore, it is best to protect yourself from this peril by developing a habit of saving.

You can be happy living simply. Buy only items that fulfil your needs and those that are necessary for your profession. For example, if you are a cameraman, you might have to buy the best camera to keep you ahead of the competition. But if you want to buy a watch, do not go for the diamond-studded one just to show off and satisfy your pride. Buy a simple watch that does its job well. When spending, see to it that the purchase adds value and does not become an indulgence. As the saying goes, 'A rupee saved is a rupee earned.'

Take a pause and think for a moment on how much money you have wasted in indulgence—money which you could have saved and used for meaningful causes, such as feeding the poor and serving the needy. It is still not too late to start saving. Small changes in lifestyle can help you achieve your financial goals. Let us see how to go about it.

Keep a record of income and expenditure for three months. The first thing to know, in fine detail, is where you spend money. Write down the expenses, both big and small, fixed and variable for three months. At the end of the first month, you will be surprised to see how much more you expend than you thought. This habit of account keeping will help you determine your spending habits, which can then be curtailed to start saving.

Let us see what a good breakdown of your net monthly income could be.

Fixed expenses every month—50 per cent. Try to limit your fixed expenses, including rent, mortgage, loans, groceries, different bills, insurance premiums, transportation and school fees to within 50 per cent of your take-home salary.

Some of the places where you could cut expenses are by using electricity judiciously, reducing fuel expenses, closing unwanted memberships to gyms or clubs and buying groceries when there are discounts. If these do not help, consider more economical housing with lower monthly payments, as that is one of the major fixed expenses every month.

BUT, HONEY, WE ONLY HAVE THREE ITEMS ON
OUR LIST...

Variable expenses—20 per cent. These expenses are optional and discretionary, such as upgrading your gadgets, car, vacation, dining out, movies, and the like. These are considered variable expenses. They can vary month-to-month and even year-to-year. Keep aside 20 per cent of your income for these. However, it is important to reduce or eliminate these when under financial stress, or when fixed expenses increase due to increased familial responsibilities.

Also, remember, whether it be for fixed or variable expenses, paying in cash versus a credit card will help you curb spending because you will tend not to overspend beyond your income.

Charity—10 per cent. The scriptures advise us to donate a minimum of 10 per cent of our total earnings to meaningful charitable causes. The total amount you donate does not matter; it is the percentage of your earnings that counts. A person earning ₹25,000 a month should aim to donate ₹2,500, while one earning ₹1 crore every month should donate ₹10 lakh. The goal should be to increase the percentage with age.

Savings—20 per cent. If you are able to manage monthly expenses (fixed and variable) and charitable donations with 80 per cent of your income, you will easily save 20 per cent every month. This is a good number to target for savings. In fact, investment experts recommend 'pay yourself first'. That means to keep aside 20 per cent in savings and then using the remaining 80 per cent for all other expenditures. And if you are unable to put that much aside, try decreasing your fixed or variable expenses.

You can further divide savings into cash and investments.

- **Cash savings**. This is your liquid cash, either in the bank or in hand. It is a good buffer to hedge against unforeseen expenditures and emergencies. Aim to keep an amount equal to 12 months of your monthly fixed expenses. This will come handy if you lose your job or the business slows down drastically. Cash savings may also help with periodic expenses such as car repair and home renovations.
- **Investments.** Aim to allocate about 10 per cent of your

income to investments. This can be a combination of bank deposits, real estate, mutual funds, retirement plans, and the like.

The aim is to grow this money over a period of time so that when you retire, you are left with enough money to lead a comfortable life. For example, if you start saving ₹5,000 every month at the age of 25 and invest it smartly, earning a Compound Annual Growth Rate (CAGR) of about 9 per cent, you would have accumulated about ₹1.47 crore by the time you are 60.

In this way, you can judiciously divide your net monthly income. There are budgeting apps as well that help you keep track in a similar manner. Following these simple steps will help you reach your financial goals, while living a comfortable lifestyle.

67

Change Investment Preferences with Age

The joy of receiving the first pay cheque is an unforgettable experience for most people. It gives a sense of achievement after years of hard work in school and college. Almost everybody plans well in advance on how to spend the initial pay cheque, and the plan is usually executed successfully.

But after the first month, the same zeal of planning should be directed towards saving and investing your money. However, that does not happen, as most youngsters are reckless with their expenses. By the time they come to their senses, they have already lost valuable years, and their finances are in a mess.

Some people do not get their investing preferences right even when they are close to retirement. But that is not how it should be. Every salary should take you one step closer to financial security. And yet, the way you invest in the twenties will be completely opposite to how you invest in your sixties. Let us see how your investment strategy should change as you age.

In the twenties, young adults should first inculcate a habit of saving. Starting early with your savings and investments is a brilliant move. You can maximize on the compounding effect of interest, where you earn on the principal and its interest accrued as well. Though this might require some sacrifices, if you learn to do them now, you will reap the benefits throughout your life.

Money management experts recommend diversifying your investment portfolio. Asset allocation should include both cash and investment. Keep aside at least six to nine months of your average monthly expenses as liquid cash or in the bank. Then, invest most of your monthly savings (80–90 per cent) in securities such as stocks, bonds and mutual funds.

You can take small, calculated risks in the stock market when young. Though they are not the safest security type, they provide higher returns over the long-term. Another benefit is that unlike a property, you do not need a large sum to invest in the stock market. Mutual funds are another great investment vehicle, as they are a combination of stocks and bonds.

You could also save in your provident fund. It is backed by the Indian government, and hence risk-free. The tax advantages are: 1) Your contribution to your provident fund of up to ₹1.5 lakh per annum is deductible from your taxable income. 2) The interest you earn is non-taxable. And, 3) the maturity amount you get after 15 years is also non-taxable.

If in the US, there are several investment vehicles designed to help you save for retirement. Look into investing in Individual Retirement Accounts (IRAs) of different kinds, 401(k)s and 403(b) plans. Many times, the employer matches a certain percentage of your contribution, and the amount is deducted from your taxable income. Likewise, the Indian government has the Employees Provident Fund (EPF) scheme. Similar government programmes exist in most countries.

Get health coverage for your family and you. Sickness in the family is not only mentally disturbing, it can also play havoc with your finances. If you are the only earning member in the family, then a life insurance will be a safety net that can come handy. Securing both health and life insurance at a young age allows you to take advantage of the low premiums, which may increase as you age.

Keep some money aside for upgrading your skills. Careers today require regular upskilling to keep up with the latest technologies and advancements. Further, if you decide to change careers, it is important to have some money available to get a new degree or certification.

After entering the thirties, life takes a major turn as most people get married in this age bracket. Expenses increase, but luckily salaries are also higher. By now, most people have settled in the line of work they are interested in, and the city they want to work in. So, it is a good time to explore the option of buying a home.

Continue investing in your portfolio of securities and cash. Consider changing the asset allocation though. From your savings, invest about 80 per cent in mutual funds or stocks (if you have gained some knowledge in it), and keep the rest in fixed deposits (FDs; also known as certificate of deposit, CDs, in the US). Alternatively, you can put money in your retirement account.

If you have children, consider opting for long-term investment schemes for them. These will help when money is needed for their education and other expenses. Discuss these options with a financial institution or your financial advisor.

In your forties, with a bigger pay package, you can plan to pay back your home loan ahead of time if it benefits in savings to you.

Continue with your investments in the selected schemes for your children. As you age, you should keep the risk under check. Hence, unless you are an expert at investing, you can reduce your contribution to mutual funds or stocks (or retirement plans) to 70 per cent of your savings. Keep the rest in fixed deposits.

Into your fifties, you have reached close to the pinnacle of your career. The salary package has increased further. Due to your smart investments, your children are also financially independent. They are likely to finish their studies and start their careers, earning and fending for themselves.

Your investments in mutual funds or stocks must have grown into a sizeable amount by now. You can continue investing (whether to retirement plans or securities), but reduce the percentage to less than 40–50 per cent of your savings. The rest of the money should be kept in fixed deposits because the priorities have now changed from quick growth to dependable income. With more time and less responsibilities, you should also aim to increase your contribution to charities from 10 per cent to a greater amount.

WE STARTED INVESTING EARLY IN LOTTERY
TICKETS. OUR RETIREMENT PLAN IS TO
WIN A MILLION-DOLLAR JACKPOT!

Retired life should be financially the best period of your life, as you are financially secure due to your investments done at an early age. Whatever money you have in your mutual funds or stocks should be withdrawn and invested in senior citizens savings scheme and other bank deposits. If in the US, you can systematically withdraw from your retirement plans for cash flow.

Now is not the time to think or worry about growing your money. By this time, along with the money in stocks, you already own a home, have money in fixed deposits and also have your retirement benefits.

For a rough calculation, if you started investing at 30 and managed to invest about ₹1 lakh every year into mutual funds, earning a 10 per cent CAGR, then by the time you retire, you would have over ₹1.6 crore.

If you were a smart investor who managed to earn a CAGR of 14 per cent on your investments, then you would have over ₹3.5 crore. If you invested more, then the final sum is likely to be much higher.

Your hard work has paid off and you are financially secure. Even if a conservative sum of ₹3 crore is taken, at a 7 per cent bank interest, you would earn about ₹21 lakh every year.

Remember, financially, **there should be three stages in life: learn, earn and return.** Until you got the job, you were dedicated to learning. Then, your focus shifted to earning. Now, it must be followed by preoccupation with returning to society through charity and philanthropic pursuits.

68

Manage Debt and Become Debt Free

Indian household debt increased from ₹6.6 trillion in March 2008 to ₹43.5 trillion in March 2020. But some might say that during that period the Indian Gross Domestic Product (GDP) has also increased. True, but even measuring against percentage of GDP, the retail loans have increased from 13.2 per cent of GDP to 21.2 per cent. This clearly shows that Indians are increasingly leaning on debt.

Is debt a bad thing? No! Taking debt for purchasing a house which is within your means or taking up a student loan for completing higher education are smart decisions.

However, the problem begins when people start loading up on debt to buy things to satisfy their senses or to maintain a certain status in society. The urge to buy the latest car, superfluous gadgets, branded clothes and recreational holidays can quickly add to debt-mountain that can become unmanageable.

In the midst of all this, if you lose your job, then missed EMI payments quickly pile up. That can stress you out and take a toll on your health and family life. Hence, before it is too late, control your debt and aim to become debt-free.

How much debt is too much? In order to assess your situation, calculate the debt-to-income ratio. This would give you the total percentage of money from your income that you spend on repaying debt.

Add all the debts you have such as home loan, student loan, personal loan and credit card loan payments. Suppose all this adds up to ₹40,000 per month and you earn ₹1 lakh a month.

Your debt-to-income ratio = (Total monthly debt payment/ Monthly income) x 100

So, in this case it is (40,000/1,00,000) x 100 = 40 per cent.

This means that out of every rupee you earn, 40 paise go for repaying your debt, which puts you in the category of excessive debt. Experts suggest keeping the debt-to-income ratio to less than 36 per cent, if it includes a home loan. But if you do not have a home loan, then the recommended ratio is below 20 per cent.

Sit down, be true to yourself and calculate your debt-to-income ratio. If it is on the higher side, do not panic. Take control of the situation.

Once established that the debt is high, what next? The first thing you need to do is to stop the activities that have put you in debt.

Suppose you are crazy about cars. No matter how many of them you own, there will always be that one car that you do not have and deeply desire. And in today's world, numerous models are released every year. So, if you get caught in that rut, you will keep buying new cars and increasing your auto loan, without long-term satisfaction.

This applies to everything in life such as visiting new places, buying smartphones or other gizmos, a new wardrobe and jewellery. When you stop the activity that has increased your debt, it will immediately halt unnecessary spending and accumulation of more debt.

While this solves one problem, you have still not started repaying your debt. Let us look into that now.

Pay off the loans that charge you the highest interest rate. This is also popular as the 'debt avalanche method'. Collate the total debts you have and the interest you pay on them. First tackle the loan that charges you the maximum interest rate, which is likely to be a credit card or a personal loan. While keeping the payments on the other loans at minimum, dedicate additional funds to paying off this debt.

There is another popular method dubbed 'debt snowball strategy', which recommends tackling the smallest debt first and then moving up the ladder. While this might be good in terms of boosting confidence, it might not be the best strategy financially. If your biggest loan also happens to be the highest interest charging, then you will end up paying a large amount of interest for a longer time.

Now, supposing you go for the debt avalanche method, where will you get the money to repay your debts?

Save. Other than your basic needs—food, rent, school fees, etc.—view all other expenditures critically. It might hurt you for the first couple of months, but it can be done.

If you use your car to go to the neighbourhood shop, stop doing so. Walk down. It might seem inconsequential, but that is how savings add up. If no one watches television at home, then cut down the cable connection or take a cheaper one that fulfils the requirement. Cut down on outings. And it may be time to stop that costly gym membership, which you had taken but did not utilize for the past year. Stop the drinking, smoking or eating out habit. Look for other similar expenses and either reduce or drop them.

Here, it might not be your decision alone because the support of your spouse and children is necessary. You should include them in the decision-making process and gather their input. Going all alone without the support of the family might not lead to success.

Generate additional income. If only one person is working, then the other might also look for an opportunity to start earning, which will be a huge support.

However, if both are already earning, then consider a side business to generate extra income. This could be as simple as tutoring children, consulting, online teaching, freelancing, real estate and other avenues in line with your talent and interest.

Next, use the annual or quarterly bonus, a pay hike, or any other monetary reward that you receive to pay down the debt. Get out of your comfort zone and challenge yourself—you will be surprised by what you are capable of.

If you are burdened under a mountain of debt, it will be a long and laborious process, but the end result will be worth it. On bringing down your debt to manageable levels, or even better, on becoming debt-free, you can productively use your time and money.

Lastly, change your lifestyle to never fall into the debt trap again. If you cannot control swiping the credit card for everything on offer, just surrender it and start using your debit card.

Take a debt only when you are trying to build an asset such as a home or land. Do not take debt for vacations or purchases. Taking a loan is easy, but returning it is the difficult part. Therefore, stay out of debt, lead a peaceful life and use your energy for meaningful endeavours.

The only debt that cannot be paid back is for the spiritual knowledge that your Guru bestows upon you. All other debts can be managed.

69

Share Your Wealth

Five hundred years ago, Saint Kabir said:

dān diye dhan nā ghaṭe, nadī ghaṭe na nīr
apanī āṅkh dekh lo, yoṅ kyā kahe kabīr

'A river does not become smaller by allowing others to use its water; nor does your wealth reduce when you give in charity. I am not telling this without a basis; see it for yourself in the world.'

The more you give, the more you receive. This is an uncommonly known divine law of the universe. What is the logic behind it? Ultimately, the whole world and everything in it belongs to God. We are only caretakers of our belongings on His behalf. **When we start serving others with what we have, we attract His divine grace.** This fills us with more of what we gave away.

Hence, never be miserly when opportunities to serve present themselves. If you are blessed with knowledge, start distributing it and you will find your own knowledge growing miraculously. If you nurture others' health, you will discover your own health becoming more robust. In whatever way possible, develop the spirit of service in your life.

When God blesses you financially, do not raise your
standard of living. Raise your standard of giving.
　　　—Mark Batterson, American author and pastor

The two viewpoints of life. When it comes to giving, there are
two kinds of people. Some subscribe to the philosophy that life
is an ice cream—it is meant to be enjoyed before it melts. They
indulge in self-gratification with all their resources, without
the sense of helping others. Their generosity is confined to
themselves, either for enjoyment or for enhancing their assets.

In contrast are those who see life as a candle that illumines until
it melts. These magnanimous people look for opportunities to
serve others as long as they live. With kindness and magnanimity,
they become invaluable contributors to those around them and
to humankind at large. This should be our philosophy of life.

The opportunities to serve the needy are unlimited. All we
require is the will to do so, and the ideas will pour forth.

The easiest way to serve is by sharing your wealth. Someone
aptly said that money is very much like cow dung—if you pile
it up, it smells. But if you spread it around, it helps other things
grow. It can reach where you cannot—to feed the hungry, nurse
the sick, clothe the poor and shelter the weak.

Some live by the principle: *chamadī jāye, par damadī na jāye*
'Let my skin (life) go, but never my wealth.' They are the
unfortunate ones, for they do not realize that by not giving,
they are hurting their own selves. Why is that so? Because in
earning money, we unknowingly hurt others or even behave in
less than proper ways. Thus, the wealth we accrue is impure. If

we do not purify it through charity, Creation makes us repay for the sins we committed in accumulating it and takes it away through doctors' bills and lawyers' fees. Hence, to purify our wealth, the Vedic scriptures instruct us to give away 10 per cent of our earnings to charity.

nyāyopārjita vittasya daśamānśhena dhīmataḥ
kartavyo viniyogaśhcha īśhvara prityarthameva cha

(*Skanda Puran*)

'Whatever you earn by lawful means, consider it your duty to offer 10 per cent of it in the service of God and humankind.'

Do not wait for affluence before you start giving. I often hear people say that they will become charitable, not in the present, but in future, when they become more prosperous. Such people fool themselves. If they do not make a habit of giving at the beginning of their career, most likely they will not give when they become wealthy either. That is because giving does not happen from the top of your bank account but from the bottom of your heart.

Sharing your earnings will make you a karm yogi. If you are like most people, you probably spend a major portion of your day at work. Thus, if you wish to progress rapidly in your spiritual journey, it is important to learn how to work in divine consciousness. For this, the Bhagavad Gita teaches the practice of karm yog, which is to remember God alongside performing your worldly duties.

However, karm yog seems to be easier said than done, because when we work, it is natural to absorb our mind in the task.

Where is the scope for concomitantly thinking of God? Well, let me share with you the simplest technique for practising it.

The major fruit of our work is the money we earn. When we offer a reasonable portion of it to God, our attitude to work naturally changes. We develop the consciousness, 'I am working as a service to the Lord. The rewards of my toil are for His pleasure. Therefore, let me strive harder, and earn more, so that I can serve even more.' In this way, giving in charity helps us easily inculcate the spirit of karm yog in our professional life.

Superior and inferior charity. The Bhagavad Gita explains that when charity is offered freely from the heart to worthy recipients, at the proper time and the appropriate place, it is in the mode of goodness. This includes donating time and money for good causes such as helping feed the needy, providing healthcare for the poor, facilitating education for the underprivileged, and so forth.

On the other hand, charity given with reluctance, with the hope of reward, is said to be in the mode of passion. And finally, charity given at the wrong place and time to unworthy persons is in the mode of ignorance.

For example, suppose money is offered to a drug addict. He uses it to get intoxicated, and then ends up committing a crime. He will definitely be punished according to the Law of Karma, but the person who gave the charity will also be culpable for the offence.

While material charity is done for the welfare of the body and helps others temporarily, the Guru is engaged in divine charity. He helps eliminate the root cause of all suffering, which is separation of the soul from God. Forgetfulness of God is, after all, the reason we are here in the world of maya, which is an ocean of suffering. Hence, assisting the Guru in his divine mission is the highest form of charity. By engaging in it, we attract divine grace and progress towards the supreme goal of life, which is God-realization.

Finally, the last word on the topic of charity. From a spiritual perspective, wealth is a shakti of God. It is an extension of the Divine Shakti, Mother Lakshmi.

Our attitude to Lakshmi should be like that of King Janak, not like Ravan. Ravan saw Mother Sita as an object of enjoyment and wanted to adopt Her as his wife. He did not respect the fact that She belonged to Lord Ram, the Master of the universe. Thus, he did not even hesitate to kidnap Her. That is why we label him as a demon. The complete reverse of Ravan was the sentiment of King Janak. He raised Sita as his daughter, with loving devotion, knowing all along that She belonged to someone else.

Similarly, in material consciousness, we think, 'I am the lord of my wealth, and I must use it for my enjoyment.' But spirituality teaches us to cultivate the noble attitude of service, 'All I have belongs to God. Whatever remains after fulfilling my necessities, I will give it away in His service.' Therefore, to grow in virtue and devotion, share your wealth generously in ways that please God.

Epilogue

L ife is God's most beautiful gift to us. Yet, most people
never live life to the fullest. Not because they don't want
to but because they don't know how to. Succeeding at life
requires deliberate effort and the proper knowledge. Einstein
defined doing the same thing over and over again and expecting
different results as insanity. And unknowingly, most of us are
living insane lives. We keep repeating the same unproductive
thinking patterns, react ineffectively in situations and forge a
less-than-ideal destiny for ourselves. If, instead, we want to
live our best life, we must change what we are doing. We must
adopt an illumined way of living. And for that, we must acquire
the best possible wisdom.

That's exactly what the successful do. They do not live
whimsically; they live by wisdom. The right knowledge
unleashes our abilities and manifests our potential to succeed
in our pursuits. This holds true in every domain of our lives.
This book is an attempt to enrich the quality of your life by
equipping you with tools in the realm of spirituality, health,
relationships, profession and finances. Keeping in mind the
dilemmas and predicaments of modern times, I selected the
topics most relevant to everyone's life. I hope it will serve as
a comprehensive manual, replete with life lessons. If we can
successfully master our physical, personal, professional and

spiritual well-being, we will win the game of life.

Hopefully, these teachings have inspired and empowered you to live your best life. When our doubts are annihilated and the mind is disciplined, we can rise from the mundane to the sublime. We can navigate through life, not haphazardly, but in an enlightened manner.

You now have various techniques to address the quandaries that show up every day. Not only can you now make good choices, but you can also live more purposefully. You can reform, embellish and beautify your life's experiences through awareness and practise.

Do not let life just happen to you. Life is a do-it-yourself project. And you need to build it with intentional and guided effort for it to flourish.

Guide to Hindi Pronunciation

Vowels

अ	*a*	as *u* in 'but'
आ	*ā*	as *a* in 'far'
इ	*i*	as *i* in 'pin'
ई	*ī*	as *i* in 'machine'
उ	*u*	as *u* in 'push'
ऊ	*ū*	as *o* in 'move'
ए	*e*	as *a* in 'evade'
ऐ	*ai*	as *a* in 'mat'; sometimes as *ai* in 'aisle' with the only difference that *a* should be pronounced as *u* in 'but', not as *a* in 'far'
ओ	*o*	as *o* in 'go'
औ	*au*	as *o* in 'pot' or as *aw* in 'saw'
ऋ	*ṛi*	as *ri* in 'Krishna'[31]
ॠ	*ṝī*	as *ree* in 'spree'

---

[31]Across the many states of India, *ṛi* is pronounced as *ru* as *u* in push. In most parts of North India, *ṛi* is pronounced as *ri* in Krishna. We have used the North Indian style here.

Consonants

Gutturals: Pronounced from the throat

क	*ka*	as *k* in 'kite'
ख	*kha*	as *kh* in 'Eckhart'
ग	*ga*	as *g* in 'goat'
घ	*gha*	as *gh* in 'dighard'
ङ	*ṅa*	as *n* in 'finger'

Palatals: Pronounced with the middle of the tongue against the palate

च	*cha*	as *ch* in 'chanel'
छ	*chha*	as *chh* in 'staunchheart'
ज	*ja*	as *j* in 'jar'
झ	*jha*	as *dgeh* in 'hedgehog'
ञ	*ña*	as *n* in 'lunch'

Cerebrals: Pronounced with the tip of the tongue against the palate

ट	*ta*	as *t* in 'tub'
ठ	*ṭha*	as *th* in 'hothead'
ड	*ḍa*	as *d* in 'divine'
ढ	*ḍha*	as *dh* in 'redhead'
ण	*ṇa*	as *n* in 'burnt'

Dentals: Pronounced like the cerebrals but with the tongue against the teeth

त	*ta*	as *t* in French word 'matron'
थ	*tha*	as *th* in 'ether'

द	*da*	as *th* in 'either'
ध	*dha*	as *dh* in 'Buddha'
न	*na*	as *n* in 'no'

Labials: Pronounced with the lips

प	*pa*	as *p* in 'pink'
फ	*pha*	as *ph* in 'uphill'
ब	*ba*	as *b* in 'boy'
भ	*bha*	as *bh* in 'abhor'
म	*ma*	as *m* in 'man'

Semivowels

य	*ya*	as *y* in 'yes'
र	*ra*	as *r* in 'remember'
ल	*la*	as *l* in 'light'
व	*va*	as *v* in 'vine', as *w* in 'swan'

Sibilants

श	*śha*	as *sh* in 'shape'
ष	*ṣha*	as *sh* in 'show'
स	*sa*	as *s* in 'sin'

Aspirate

ह	*ha*	as *h* in 'hut'

Visarga

:	*ḥ*	it is a strong aspirate; also lengthens the preceding vowel and occurs only at the end of a word. It is pronounced as a final *h* sound

Anusvara Nasalized

̇	ṁ/ṅ	nasalizes and lengthens the preceding vowel and is pronounced as *n* in the words 'and' or 'anthem'[32]
̐	~	as *n* in 'gung-ho'

Avagraha

S	'	This is a silent character indicating अ. It is written but not pronounced; used in specific combination (sandhi) rules

Others

क्ष	kṣha	as *ksh* in 'freakshow'
ज्ञ	jña	as *gy* in 'bigyoung'
ड़	ṛa	There is no sign in English to represent the sound ड़. It has been written as *ṛa* but the tip of the tongue quickly flaps down
ढ़	ṛha	There is no sign in English to represent the sound ढ़. It has been written as *ṛha*, but the tip of the tongue quickly flaps down

---

[32]Sometimes nasalized and sometimes not. In many words such as *Aṁsh, Saṁskar,* etc. are pronounced with a nasal sound as *Aṅsh, Saṅskar,* etc. Since it is nasalized, we are using *ṅ*.

Glossary

Abhiniveśh	fear of death; separation from everything we hold dear; clinging to the things around us
Āmlā	Indian gooseberry
Āratī	a hymn which is all about the glories of God
Asan	sitting or standing posture; generally used in yoga
Auṣhadhi	medicine
Bhagavan	Supreme Lord, who is the possessor of infinite opulences
Bhajans	devotional hymns
Bhakti	devotion; love for God
Bhav	sentiments
Bhav-rog patients	souls afflicted by maya
Brahma Muhūrt	also known as the Creator's time. Approximately, the last two hours of the night immediately preceding sunrise
Brahmānand	bliss of the formless aspect of God
Buddhi Yog	yog of the intellect; science of using one's intellect to rein the urges of the mind and senses
Chintan	contemplation; to repeatedly revise a piece of knowledge in the mind and intellect

Dhan	wealth
Dhobi	washerman or laundryman
Dhyan	meditation
Eudaemonia	of Greek origin; lasting satisfaction that comes from accomplishment
Guru-bhais	disciples of the same Guru
Hedonia	of Greek origin; short-lived enjoyment
Japa mala	rosary beads used for chanting
Japa	chanting of Names of God
Kāḍhā	a hot medicinal drink made by boiling select herbs and spices in water
Kaizen	Japanese philosophy of continuous improvement
Karm yog	as explained in the Bhagavad Gita, the act of doing your worldly tasks with the mind attached to God
Kirtans	hearing, singing and remembering the Names, Forms, Qualities, Pastimes, Abodes and Associates of God; usually done in a group
Leelas	Pastimes of God
Man	mind
Manan	see *chintan*
Mānas rog	mental afflictions. According to the Vedic scriptures, sentiments of anger, jealousy, greed, revenge, desire, pride, etc.
Mānasī sevā	serving God in the mind, by thought
Maya	God's insentient material energy from which this world is created

Nididhyāsan	internalize a concept with firm faith
Nirvikalpa samadhi	state of samadhi characterized by thoughtlessness
Niṣhkām bhakti	selfless devotion; worship with the aim of serving God for His happiness alone
Pranayam	practice of breath regulation
Prārthanā	prayer
Premānand	bliss of the personal form of God
Preya	happiness that is immensely sweet at first, but later turns into poison
Rajasic	one of the three modes of material nature; of the mode of passion
Roop Dhyan	a meditation technique propagated by Jagadguru Kripaluji Maharaj in which the meditator sits with eyes closed and focuses on an image or images of any form of God
Sādhaks	spiritual aspirants
Sadhana	spiritual practice, usually done daily
Samadhi	a state of intense concentration achieved through meditation
Sanskārs	accumulated tendencies from endless previous lifetimes
Satsang	association that takes our mind to the Absolute Truth and purifies our mind
Sattvic	one of the three modes of material nature; of the mode of goodness
Sevā bhav	the sentiment or attitude of service
Śhraddhā	faith

Śhravaṇ	to hear or read divine or spiritual knowledge
Śhreya	happiness that initially seems like poison, but later becomes like nectar
Tamasic	one of the three modes of material nature; of the mode of ignorance
Tan	body
Tulsi	holy basil
Yog	from Sanskrit root 'yuj' meaning to join; union of our tiny soul with the Supreme Soul (God)

Let's Connect

If you enjoyed reading this book and would like to connect with Swami Mukundananda, you can reach him through any of the following channels:

Websites: *www.jkyog.org, www.jkyog.in, www.swamimukundananda.org*

YouTube channels: 'Swami Mukundananda' and 'Swami Mukundananda Hindi'

Facebook: 'Swami Mukundananda' and 'Swami Mukundananda Hindi'

Instagram: 'Swami Mukundananda' and 'Swami Mukundananda Hindi'

Pinterest: Swami Mukundananda - JKYog

Telegram: Swami Mukundananda

Twitter: Swami Mukundananda (@Sw_Mukundananda)

LinkedIn: Swami Mukundananda

Podcasts: Apple, Google, SoundCloud, Spotify, Stitcher

JKYog Radio: TuneIn app for iOS and Android

JKYog App: Available for iOS and Android

WhatsApp Daily Inspirations: We have two broadcast lists. You are welcome to join either or both.

India: +91 84489 41008
USA: +1 346-239-9675

Online Classes:

JKYog India: *www.jkyog.in/online-sessions/*
JKYog US: *www.jkyog.org/online-classes*

Email: deskofswamiji@swamimukundananda.org

To bring *Golden Rules for Living Your Best Life* or Swami Mukundananda to your organization—as Google, Intel, Oracle, Verizon, United Nations, Stanford University, Yale University, IITs and IIMs have done—look us up at *sm-leadership.org* or write to us at info@sm-leadership.org.